AF413606

OVERCOMING THE TRAP OF OVERTHINKING

STOP OVERTHINKING

AMIT GUPTA

Contents

Acknowledgements

I extend my deepest gratitude to all those who have contributed to the creation of this comprehensive exploration into overcoming overthinking and nurturing mindfulness and self-awareness.

First and foremost, I would like to express my appreciation to the countless authors, researchers, and practitioners whose insights, wisdom, and teachings have informed and inspired the content of this work. Their dedication to understanding the complexities of the human mind and promoting well-being has laid the foundation for our exploration into these transformative topics.

I am indebted to the individuals who have shared their personal stories, struggles, and triumphs with overthinking, mindfulness, and self-awareness. Your courage, vulnerability, and resilience serve as a beacon of hope and inspiration for others on their journey of self-discovery and growth.

I am grateful to the teachers, mentors, and guides who have imparted their knowledge, wisdom, and guidance in the realms of mindfulness, meditation, and self-awareness. Your unwavering support, encouragement, and insight have been instrumental in shaping the content of this work and fostering a deeper understanding of these profound practices.

I would also like to thank my friends, family members, and loved ones for their unwavering support, encouragement, and understanding throughout the process of creating this work. Your love, patience, and belief in me have been a source of strength and inspiration, fueling my passion for personal growth and well-being.

Last but not least, I express my heartfelt appreciation to the readers who have embarked on this journey of exploration and discovery. May the insights, reflections, and practices shared in this work serve as a guiding light on your path to overcoming overthinking, nurturing mindfulness, and cultivating self-awareness. Your willingness to engage in this transformative journey is a testament to your courage, resilience, and commitment to living a life of meaning, purpose, and authenticity.

With gratitude and humility,

The Author

Hello, and welcome. My name is Amit, and I'm delighted to have this opportunity to share a bit about myself with you.

But writing is more than just a craft for me; it's a calling, a path of growth and transformation. Through my words, I strive to inspire, empower, and uplift others on their own journeys of self-discovery and personal growth.

My hope is that my work resonates with you, that it speaks to the depths of your being and stirs something within you. Whether you find solace in the pages of my poetry, guidance in the wisdom of my prose, or inspiration in the stories I share, know that you are not alone on this journey.

We are fellow travelers on the winding road of life, navigating its twists and turns, its joys and sorrows, together. And through the power of storytelling, we can find solace, strength, and solidarity in each other's experiences.

So, thank you for joining me here today, for allowing me to share a glimpse of my world with you. And as we continue on our respective journeys, may we find beauty in the ordinary, wisdom in the unknown, and courage in the face of adversity.

CHAPTER ONE

1.1 The Paralysis of Analysis

Introduction

In this chapter, we delve into the intricate web of overthinking, beginning with an exploration of its fundamental nature: the paralysis of analysis. Overthinking, a common affliction for many, traps individuals in a cycle of relentless rumination, hindering decision-making and causing undue stress and anxiety. By understanding the roots of this phenomenon, we can begin to unravel its grip and reclaim control over our thoughts and actions.

Defining Overthinking

Overthinking can be defined as the excessive and repetitive dwelling on thoughts, often leading to indecision and inaction. It encompasses a range of cognitive processes, including overanalyzing past events, worrying about the future, and scrutinizing every detail of present circumstances. While some degree of reflection is natural and beneficial, overthinking crosses the line into detrimental territory, impairing one's ability to function effectively.

Understanding the Roots

The roots of overthinking can be traced to various psychological and environmental factors. Perfectionism, fear of failure, and a need for control are common contributors, driving individuals to incessantly analyze situations in search of the perfect solution. Moreover, past experiences of trauma or rejection can fuel a cycle of negative thought patterns, perpetuating the cycle of overthinking.

The Psychological Impact

The psychological impact of overthinking is profound, manifesting in heightened levels of stress, anxiety, and self-doubt. The constant barrage of thoughts creates a sense of mental clutter, making it difficult to focus or find clarity. As a result, individuals may feel overwhelmed, trapped in a state of perpetual indecision, and unable to move forward.

Recognizing the Signs

Recognizing the signs of overthinking is the first step toward breaking free from its grip. Common indicators include excessive rumination, second-guessing oneself, and difficulty making decisions. Physical symptoms such as tension headaches, insomnia, and fatigue may also accompany prolonged periods of overthinking, further exacerbating the problem.

Breaking the Cycle

Breaking free from the paralysis of analysis requires a

multi-faceted approach. By identifying triggers and thought patterns, individuals can begin to challenge the validity of their thoughts and cultivate more adaptive coping strategies. Cognitive behavioral techniques, mindfulness practices, and stress management strategies all play a vital role in interrupting the cycle of overthinking and promoting mental well-being.

Conclusion

In conclusion, the paralysis of analysis represents a significant barrier to living a fulfilling and balanced life. By understanding its underlying mechanisms and recognizing its signs, individuals can begin to reclaim control over their thoughts and actions. Through deliberate practice and a commitment to self-awareness, it is possible to break free from the cycle of overthinking and embrace a more mindful and purposeful way of being.

1.2 Introduction to Overthinking: Defining the Problem

Overthinking is a common phenomenon that affects individuals across all walks of life. It is characterized by the tendency to dwell excessively on thoughts, often leading to indecision, anxiety, and stress. In this chapter, we delve into the intricacies of overthinking, exploring its definition, causes, and consequences.

Defining Overthinking

Overthinking can be defined as the process of obsessively analyzing and re-analyzing a situation, problem, or thought. It involves dwelling on past events, worrying about the future, or excessively focusing on present circumstances. While some degree of reflection is natural and can be beneficial, overthinking crosses the line into harmful territory when it becomes repetitive, intrusive, and impedes one's ability to function effectively.

The Complexity of Overthinking

The complexity of overthinking lies in its multi-faceted nature. It can manifest in various forms, such as rumination, catastrophizing, and analysis paralysis. Rumination involves repetitively thinking about past events or mistakes, often leading to feelings of regret or sadness. Catastrophizing involves imagining the worst-case scenarios and blowing things out of proportion. Analysis paralysis refers to the inability to make decisions due to excessive analysis and overthinking.

Causes of Overthinking

Several factors contribute to the development of overthinking tendencies. Perfectionism, fear of failure, and a need for control are common underlying causes. Individuals who hold themselves to unrealistically high standards may find themselves trapped in a cycle of overthinking as they strive for perfection in every aspect of their lives. Similarly, a fear of failure or making mistakes can lead to constant second-guessing and overanalyzing. Environmental factors such as childhood experiences, societal pressures, and cultural norms can also influence one's propensity for overthinking. Growing up in an environment where mistakes are heavily criticized or where success is equated with perfection can contribute to the development of overthinking patterns. Likewise, societal pressures to excel in every area of life and cultural norms that prioritize productivity and achievement can exacerbate overthinking tendencies.

Consequences of Overthinking

The consequences of overthinking can be far-reaching, impacting various aspects of an individual's life. From relationships to work performance to mental and physical health, overthinking can take a significant toll. In relationships, overthinking can lead to communication breakdowns, insecurity, and conflict. In the workplace, it can result in decreased productivity, missed opportunities, and burnout. On a personal level, overthinking can contribute to anxiety disorders, depression, and other mental health issues.

Recognizing Overthinking

Recognizing the signs of overthinking is the first step toward addressing the problem. Common indicators include excessive worrying, difficulty making decisions, repetitive thoughts, and physical symptoms such as tension headaches or insomnia. By becoming more aware of these signs, individuals can begin to take proactive steps to manage their overthinking tendencies and reduce its impact on their lives.

Conclusion

In conclusion, overthinking is a pervasive issue that affects millions of people worldwide. It is characterized by excessive rumination, indecision, and anxiety and can have profound consequences on various aspects of an individual's life. By understanding the complexities of overthinking, including its causes and consequences, individuals can begin to take steps to address the problem and reclaim control over their thoughts and actions.

1.3 Understanding the Roots of Overthinking

Introduction

In this chapter, we delve into the underlying causes and origins of overthinking. By understanding the roots of this pervasive phenomenon, we can gain insight into why it occurs and how it manifests in our thoughts and behaviors.

Perfectionism: A Common Culprit

One of the primary roots of overthinking is perfectionism. Perfectionists set unrealistically high standards for themselves and fear making mistakes or falling short of expectations. As a result, they engage in excessive analysis and rumination, constantly striving for flawlessness in every aspect of their lives.

Fear of Failure

Another significant contributor to overthinking is the fear of failure. Individuals who are afraid of failing often engage in repetitive thinking patterns, obsessively analyzing past mistakes or potential pitfalls. This fear can paralyze individuals, preventing them from taking risks or making decisions out of fear of making the wrong choice.

Need for Control

The need for control is also closely linked to overthinking. Individuals who feel a strong need to control every aspect of their lives may engage in excessive planning, rumination, and analysis in an attempt to predict and manage outcomes. However, this need for control can ultimately backfire, leading to increased stress and anxiety.

Childhood Experiences

Childhood experiences play a significant role in shaping our patterns of thinking and behavior, including overthinking tendencies. Growing up in an environment where mistakes are heavily criticized or where success is equated with perfection can contribute to the development of overthinking patterns later in life.

Societal Pressures

Societal pressures, such as the expectation to excel in every area of life, can also fuel overthinking. In a culture that values productivity and achievement, individuals may feel compelled to constantly strive for success, leading to heightened levels of stress and anxiety.

Trauma and Rejection

Past experiences of trauma or rejection can also contribute to the development of overthinking tendencies. Individuals who have experienced significant setbacks or rejections may engage in repetitive thinking patterns as a way to cope with unresolved emotions or to protect themselves from future harm.

Genetic and Biological Factors

Recent research suggests that genetic and biological factors may also play a role in predisposing individuals to overthinking. Certain genetic variations and neurotransmitter imbalances have been linked to increased levels of anxiety and rumination, which are hallmark features of overthinking.

Environmental Influences

Environmental factors, such as job stress, financial instability, or relationship conflicts, can exacerbate overthinking tendencies. When faced with challenging circumstances, individuals may engage in heightened levels of rumination and analysis in an attempt to regain a sense of control or find a solution to their problems.

Conclusion

In conclusion, the roots of overthinking are complex and multi-faceted, encompassing a range of psychological, environmental, and biological factors. By understanding these underlying causes, individuals can gain insight into why they engage in overthinking and begin to address these root issues in order to break free from its grip.

1.4 the Psychological Impact: Anxiety, Stress, and Indecision

Introduction

Overthinking, a common phenomenon experienced by individuals across all walks of life, often leads to a range of negative psychological consequences. In this comprehensive exploration, we delve into the intricate interplay between overthinking and its psychological impact, focusing on the debilitating effects of anxiety, stress, and indecision. By understanding the psychological toll of overthinking, we can begin to recognize the urgency of addressing this pervasive issue and explore strategies for mitigating its harmful effects.

Understanding Anxiety

Anxiety is a pervasive emotional state characterized by feelings of apprehension, worry, and nervousness. For individuals prone to overthinking, anxiety often becomes a constant companion, fueled by incessant rumination and catastrophic thinking patterns. The relentless scrutiny of past events, anticipation of future outcomes, and fixation on potential threats contribute to a heightened sense of unease and apprehension.

Overthinkers may find themselves trapped in a cycle of "what if" scenarios, imagining the worst-case outcomes of every decision or action. This catastrophizing mindset amplifies feelings of anxiety, leading to a pervasive sense of dread and impending doom. As anxiety levels escalate, individuals may experience physical symptoms such as rapid heartbeat, shortness of breath, and muscle tension, further exacerbating their distress.

The Impact of Stress

Stress, a natural response to perceived threats or challenges, becomes magnified in the context of overthinking. The constant barrage of intrusive thoughts and relentless analysis creates a state of chronic stress, overwhelming the body's natural coping mechanisms and impairing its ability to function optimally.

Overthinkers often find themselves caught in a cycle of "analysis paralysis," unable to make decisions or take action due to fear of making the wrong choice. This indecision perpetuates feelings of stress and uncertainty as individuals grapple with the consequences of their inaction. Moreover, the persistent rumination associated with overthinking consumes valuable mental and emotional resources, leaving individuals feeling mentally exhausted and emotionally drained.

The Cycle of Indecision

Indecision is a hallmark feature of overthinking, stemming from a fear of making mistakes or facing undesirable outcomes. Overthinkers are plagued by self-doubt and second-guessing, constantly weighing the pros and cons of every decision and seeking reassurance from others. This indecisiveness often leads to missed opportunities, as individuals remain stuck in a state of perpetual analysis, unable to commit to a course of action.

The cycle of indecision perpetuates feelings of frustration and self-criticism as individuals berate themselves for their inability to make choices confidently. Moreover, indecision breeds a sense of powerlessness and resignation as individuals relinquish control over their lives to the whims of uncertainty.

Cognitive Distortions and Negative Thinking Patterns

The psychological impact of overthinking is further compounded by cognitive distortions and negative thinking patterns. Overthinkers tend to engage in black-and-white thinking, viewing situations in extremes and discounting shades of gray. They may also engage in all-or-nothing thinking, perceiving minor setbacks as catastrophic failures and magnifying their significance.

Additionally, overthinkers often fall victim to the "mental filter" cognitive distortion, selectively focusing on negative aspects of a situation while ignoring positive elements. This pessimistic outlook perpetuates feelings of hopelessness and despair, reinforcing the cycle of overthinking and exacerbating its psychological impact.

Addressing the Psychological Impact: Strategies for Coping

Despite the pervasive psychological impact of overthinking, there are strategies individuals can employ to mitigate its harmful effects and cultivate greater psychological well-being.

1. **Mindfulness and Grounding Techniques**: Mindfulness

practices, such as deep breathing, meditation, and body scanning, can help individuals cultivate present-moment awareness and reduce the grip of overthinking. Grounding techniques, such as focusing on sensory experiences or engaging in physical activity, can also help individuals reconnect with the present moment and alleviate feelings of anxiety and stress.

2. **Cognitive Restructuring**: Cognitive behavioral techniques, such as cognitive restructuring, can help individuals challenge negative thinking patterns and reframe catastrophic thoughts. By identifying and disputing irrational beliefs, individuals can cultivate a more balanced and adaptive perspective, reducing the psychological impact of overthinking.

3. **Stress Management Strategies**: Stress management techniques, such as time management, prioritization, and relaxation techniques, can help individuals cope with the demands of overthinking and reduce feelings of overwhelm. By establishing healthy boundaries, setting realistic expectations, and incorporating self-care practices into their daily routine, individuals can build resilience and mitigate the psychological impact of overthinking.

4. **Decision-Making Skills**: Enhancing decision-making skills can help individuals overcome indecision and break free from the cycle of overthinking. By learning to trust their instincts, gather relevant information, and weigh the pros and cons of different options, individuals can make decisions more confidently and assertively, reducing feelings of uncertainty and doubt.

5. Seeking Support: Finally, seeking support from friends, family, or mental health professionals can provide individuals with the validation, encouragement, and guidance they need to cope with the psychological impact of overthinking. Whether through therapy, support groups, or informal conversations, sharing experiences and seeking perspective can help individuals feel less alone in their struggles and empower them to take steps toward greater psychological well-being.

Conclusion

In conclusion, the psychological impact of overthinking is profound, encompassing feelings of anxiety, stress, and indecision that can significantly impair an individual's quality of life. By understanding the mechanisms underlying these psychological effects and implementing strategies for coping and resilience, individuals can mitigate the harmful consequences of overthinking and cultivate greater psychological well-being. Through mindfulness, cognitive restructuring, stress management, decision-making skills, and seeking support, individuals can reclaim control over their thoughts and actions, breaking free from the cycle of overthinking and embracing a more balanced and fulfilling way of life.

CHAPTER TWO

Breaking Down the Patterns

Introduction

In this chapter, we embark on a journey to dissect the intricate patterns of overthinking that often ensnare individuals in a cycle of rumination and indecision. By understanding the common patterns and thought processes associated with overthinking, we can begin to unravel its grip and implement strategies for breaking free from its confines.

Recognizing Common Patterns of Overthinking

One of the first steps in overcoming overthinking is to recognize the common patterns that underlie this phenomenon. These patterns often manifest in repetitive thought loops, excessive worry, and analysis paralysis. By identifying these patterns, individuals can gain insight into their overthinking tendencies and begin to take steps toward change.

Rumination: One of the most prevalent patterns of overthinking is rumination, which involves repeatedly dwelling on past events or mistakes. This constant rehashing of past experiences can lead to feelings of regret, guilt, and self-criticism, further perpetuating the cycle of overthinking.

Catastrophizing: Another common pattern is catastrophizing, where individuals imagine the worst-case scenarios and blow things out of proportion. This negative thinking pattern can lead to heightened anxiety and a skewed perception of reality as individuals become consumed by irrational fears and anxieties.

Analysis Paralysis: Analysis paralysis refers to the inability to make decisions due to excessive analysis and overthinking. Individuals may become so overwhelmed by the multitude of options and potential outcomes that they become immobilized, unable to take action or move forward.

Identifying Triggers and Thought Loops

Understanding the triggers that precipitate episodes of overthinking is essential for breaking down these patterns. Triggers can be external, such as stressful situations or critical feedback, or internal, such as negative self-talk or perfectionistic tendencies. By identifying these triggers, individuals can learn to anticipate and manage them more effectively, reducing the likelihood of succumbing to overthinking.

Thought loops are another important aspect to consider when examining patterns of overthinking. These repetitive thought patterns often revolve around themes of self-doubt, fear, and uncertainty. By becoming aware of these thought loops, individuals can begin to challenge and reframe them, replacing negative thinking patterns with more constructive and empowering beliefs.

How Overthinking Manifests in Different Aspects of Life

Overthinking can manifest in various aspects of life, including relationships, work, and personal development. In relationships, overthinking can lead to communication breakdowns, insecurity, and conflict. Individuals may become preoccupied with interpreting the thoughts and intentions of others, leading to miscommunication and misunderstandings. In the workplace, overthinking can manifest as perfectionism, procrastination, and decision-making paralysis. Individuals may become so preoccupied with getting things right that they struggle to make decisions or take action, leading to decreased productivity and performance.

Breaking the Cycle of Overthinking

Breaking free from the cycle of overthinking requires a multi-faceted approach that addresses both the cognitive and emotional aspects of this phenomenon.

Cognitive Behavioral Techniques: Cognitive behavioral techniques, such as cognitive restructuring and thought challenging, can help individuals identify and challenge negative thinking patterns associated with overthinking. By replacing irrational beliefs with more rational and balanced ones, individuals can begin to break free from the cycle of rumination and self-doubt.

Mindfulness Practices: Mindfulness practices, such as meditation and deep breathing exercises, can help individuals cultivate present-moment awareness and reduce the grip of overthinking. By learning to observe their thoughts without judgment, individuals can gain perspective on their overthinking tendencies and develop greater emotional resilience.

Stress Management Strategies: Stress management techniques, such as time management and relaxation techniques, can help individuals cope with the demands of overthinking and reduce feelings of overwhelm. By establishing healthy boundaries and prioritizing self-care, individuals can build resilience and mitigate the harmful effects of stress.

Conclusion

In conclusion, breaking down the patterns of overthinking is essential for reclaiming control over our thoughts and actions. By recognizing common patterns, identifying triggers, and implementing strategies for change, individuals can begin to unravel the grip of overthinking and cultivate a more balanced and fulfilling way of life. Through cognitive behavioral techniques, mindfulness practices, and stress management strategies, individuals can break free from the cycle of rumination and indecision, embracing a more empowered and resilient mindset.

2.2 Recognizing Common Patterns of Overthinking

Introduction

Overthinking, a pervasive cognitive phenomenon, manifests in various patterns that can significantly impact individuals' mental well-being and decision-making abilities. In this comprehensive exploration, we delve into the intricate web of overthinking patterns, shedding light on their manifestations, underlying mechanisms, and consequences. By recognizing these common patterns, individuals can begin to unravel the grip of overthinking and cultivate more adaptive thinking habits.

The Cycle of Rumination

One of the most prevalent patterns of overthinking is rumination, characterized by repetitive and intrusive thoughts about past events or mistakes. Individuals caught in the cycle of rumination often find themselves dwelling on perceived failures or shortcomings, replaying events in their minds and fixating on what could have been done differently. This constant rehashing of past experiences not only perpetuates feelings of guilt and regret but also prevents individuals from moving forward and focusing on the present moment. Moreover, rumination tends to amplify negative emotions, leading to heightened levels of anxiety and depression.

Catastrophizing

Another common pattern of overthinking is catastrophizing, wherein individuals magnify the potential consequences of a situation, blowing things out of proportion and imagining the worst-case scenarios. Catastrophizers tend to focus on the negative aspects of a situation while discounting any positive outcomes or potential solutions. This distorted thinking pattern fuels feelings of fear and anxiety as individuals become consumed by thoughts of impending disaster. Consequently, catastrophizing can lead to avoidance behaviors and decision paralysis, as individuals are paralyzed by the fear of making a wrong choice.

Analysis Paralysis

Analysis paralysis is yet another pattern of overthinking characterized by an inability to make decisions due to excessive analysis and deliberation. Individuals caught in this pattern become overwhelmed by the multitude of options and possibilities, leading to a state of decision gridlock. Despite their best efforts to weigh the pros and cons and gather additional information, they find themselves stuck in a perpetual cycle of analysis, unable to commit to a course of action. This indecision not only wastes valuable time and mental energy but also fosters feelings of frustration and self-doubt.

Black-and-White Thinking

Black-and-white thinking, also known as dichotomous thinking, is a cognitive distortion commonly observed in individuals prone to overthinking. In this pattern, individuals view situations in extremes, categorizing them as either all good or all bad, with no room for nuance or complexity. This rigid thinking pattern fosters a polarized worldview, wherein individuals fail to recognize the shades of gray between the extremes. Consequently, they may engage in all-or-nothing behaviors, striving for perfection or avoiding situations altogether out of fear of failure.

Selective Attention

Selective attention is another cognitive bias that often accompanies overthinking, wherein individuals selectively focus on negative aspects of a situation while ignoring or downplaying positive elements. This pattern of selective attention reinforces pessimistic thinking and fosters a skewed perception of reality. Individuals may become preoccupied with perceived threats or failures, overlooking opportunities for growth or success. As a result, they may feel perpetually dissatisfied and discontented despite outward achievements or accomplishments.

Comparison and Social Comparison

Comparison and social comparison are two additional patterns of overthinking that can significantly impact individuals' self-esteem and well-being. In comparison, individuals measure themselves against others, evaluating their worth and success based on external standards or benchmarks. This constant comparison fosters feelings of inadequacy and inferiority as individuals strive to meet unattainable standards of perfection set by society or peers. In social comparison, individuals compare themselves to others within their social circle, seeking validation and approval from others. This pattern of overthinking can lead to feelings of jealousy, resentment, or inadequacy, as individuals perceive themselves as falling short in comparison to others. Moreover, social comparison fosters a sense of competition and rivalry, undermining genuine connections and fostering insecurity in relationships.

Overgeneralization

Overgeneralization is a cognitive distortion wherein individuals draw sweeping conclusions based on limited or anecdotal evidence. In the context of overthinking, individuals may extrapolate a single negative experience to apply to all future situations, leading to a distorted perception of reality. This pattern of thinking fosters pessimism and hopelessness, as individuals perceive themselves as doomed to repeat past mistakes or encounter failure at every turn.

Seeking Reassurance

Seeking reassurance is a common coping mechanism employed by individuals prone to overthinking, wherein they seek validation and approval from others to alleviate feelings of uncertainty or doubt. However, this pattern of seeking reassurance can become a maladaptive coping strategy, reinforcing dependency on external validation and perpetuating feelings of insecurity. Moreover, constant reassurance-seeking behaviors can strain relationships and undermine individuals' self-confidence and autonomy.

Conclusion

In conclusion, recognizing common patterns of overthinking is essential for understanding its underlying mechanisms and consequences. From the cycle of rumination to catastrophizing, analysis paralysis, and cognitive distortions such as black-and-white thinking and selective attention, these patterns can significantly impact individuals' mental well-being and decision-making abilities. By becoming aware of these patterns and their effects, individuals can begin to challenge maladaptive thinking habits and cultivate more adaptive ways of thinking and coping. Through mindfulness, cognitive restructuring, and self-compassion, individuals can learn to break free from the grip of overthinking and embrace a more balanced and resilient approach to life. By recognizing their inherent worth and fostering a sense of acceptance and gratitude, individuals can overcome the negative effects of overthinking and cultivate greater psychological well-being and resilience in the face of adversity.

2.3 Identifying Triggers and Thought Loops in Overthinking

Introduction

In the labyrinth of overthinking, identifying triggers and thought loops is akin to finding the keys to unlock the shackles that bind one's mind. Triggers are the catalysts that set off a chain reaction of thoughts, while thought loops are the cyclical patterns of rumination that ensnare individuals in a web of repetitive thinking. In this exploration, we delve into the intricacies of identifying triggers and thought loops in overthinking, shedding light on their origins, manifestations, and implications. By gaining insight into these phenomena, individuals can begin to unravel the complexities of their overthinking patterns and take steps toward liberation from its grasp.

Understanding Triggers

Triggers are external or internal stimuli that provoke a heightened emotional response or activate a specific thought pattern. They can take myriad forms, ranging from sensory cues to interpersonal interactions to internal thoughts and emotions. Triggers are highly individualized and may vary in intensity and frequency from person to person.

External triggers encompass a wide array of stimuli present in the individual's environment. These may include sensory cues such as sights, sounds, or smells that evoke memories or emotions. For example, a particular song playing on the radio may trigger memories of a past relationship, leading to feelings of sadness or nostalgia. Similarly, social situations or interactions with specific individuals may serve as triggers, eliciting feelings of anxiety, insecurity, or discomfort.

Internal triggers, on the other hand, arise from within the individual's own mind and body. These may include thoughts, emotions, or bodily sensations that evoke a heightened emotional response. For example, feelings of inadequacy or self-doubt may serve as internal triggers, prompting individuals to engage in rumination or negative self-talk. Likewise, physical sensations such as tension or discomfort may signal the onset of stress or anxiety, triggering a cascade of intrusive thoughts.

Identifying Thought Loops

Thought loops are the repetitive patterns of rumination that characterize overthinking. They involve the relentless cycling of thoughts around a particular theme or issue, often leading to feelings of frustration, anxiety, or helplessness. Thought loops can manifest in various forms, ranging from dwelling on past mistakes to worrying about the future to obsessing over present circumstances.

One common form of thought loop is rumination, wherein individuals become fixated on past events or mistakes, replaying them in their minds and dwelling on what could have been done differently. This constant rehashing of the past prevents individuals from moving forward and fosters feelings of regret, guilt, or self-blame.

Another common thought loop is catastrophizing, wherein individuals magnify the potential consequences of a situation, imagining the worst-case scenarios and dwelling on what could go wrong. This pattern of thinking fuels feelings of anxiety and apprehension, leading to a heightened sense of fear and uncertainty.

Breaking the Cycle

Breaking free from the cycle of overthinking requires a multi-faceted approach that involves both identifying triggers and thought loops and developing strategies to mitigate their impact. One effective strategy is mindfulness, which involves cultivating present-moment awareness and non-judgmental acceptance of one's thoughts and emotions. By learning to observe their thoughts without getting caught up in them, individuals can gain insight into their triggers and thought loops and begin to disengage from them.

Cognitive restructuring is another powerful technique for breaking the cycle of overthinking. This involves challenging negative or distorted thoughts and replacing them with more balanced and realistic alternatives. By questioning the validity of their thoughts and reframing them in a more positive light, individuals can reduce the intensity and frequency of their triggers and thought loops.

Additionally, behavioral strategies such as distraction and problem-solving can help individuals interrupt the cycle of overthinking and redirect their attention toward more constructive activities. Engaging in enjoyable or fulfilling activities, such as hobbies or exercise, can provide a welcome respite from rumination and help individuals regain a sense of perspective and control. Furthermore, seeking support from friends, family, or mental health professionals can provide individuals with validation, encouragement, and guidance in navigating their triggers and thought loops. Whether through therapy, support groups, or informal conversations, sharing experiences and seeking perspective can help individuals feel less alone in their struggles and empower them to take steps toward greater psychological well-being.

Conclusion

In conclusion, identifying triggers and thought loops is a crucial step in understanding and addressing the complexities of overthinking. Triggers are the catalysts that set off a chain reaction of thoughts and emotions, while thought loops are the cyclical patterns of rumination that ensnare individuals in a web of repetitive thinking. By gaining insight into these phenomena and developing strategies to mitigate their impact, individuals can begin to break free from the cycle of overthinking and cultivate a more balanced and resilient approach to life.

Through mindfulness, cognitive restructuring, behavioral strategies, and seeking support, individuals can learn to identify their triggers and thought loops, challenge maladaptive thinking habits, and cultivate greater psychological well-being and resilience in the face of adversity.

2.4 How Overthinking Manifests in Different Aspects of Life: Relationships, Work, and Personal Development

Introduction

Overthinking, a common cognitive pattern characterized by excessive rumination and analysis, can permeate various aspects of individuals' lives, including their relationships, work, and personal development. In this comprehensive exploration, we delve into the intricate ways in which overthinking manifests in each of these domains, shedding light on its detrimental effects and providing strategies for mitigation; by understanding how overthinking impacts different areas of life, individuals can begin to recognize its pervasive influence and take steps to cultivate healthier thinking habits.

Overthinking in Relationships

In relationships, overthinking can manifest in a multitude of ways, often leading to communication breakdowns, insecurity, and conflict. One common manifestation of overthinking is incessant rumination about past interactions or perceived slights, leading individuals to dwell on minor incidents or misunderstandings and blow them out of proportion. This pattern of overthinking can create tension and resentment within the relationship as individuals become preoccupied with grievances or perceived injustices.

Moreover, overthinking can foster feelings of insecurity and self-doubt, leading individuals to question their partner's motives or intentions. This constant scrutiny and mistrust can erode the foundation of trust and intimacy within the relationship, leading to feelings of isolation and disconnection. Additionally, overthinkers may engage in catastrophic thinking, imagining worst-case scenarios or jumping to conclusions without sufficient evidence, further exacerbating feelings of anxiety and insecurity.

In romantic relationships, overthinking can also manifest in attachment-related behaviors, such as clinginess or avoidance. Individuals prone to overthinking may become overly dependent on their partner for validation and reassurance, seeking constant affirmation of their worth and desirability. Alternatively, they may withdraw emotionally or erect walls to protect themselves from perceived rejection or abandonment.

Overthinking at Work

At the workplace, overthinking can significantly impact individuals' productivity, decision-making abilities, and overall job satisfaction. One common manifestation of overthinking in the workplace is analysis paralysis, wherein individuals become paralyzed by indecision due to excessive analysis and deliberation. Instead of taking decisive action, they may second-guess themselves or procrastinate, fearing making the wrong choice.

Moreover, overthinking can hinder individuals' ability to prioritize tasks and manage their time effectively. Constantly ruminating on past mistakes or worrying about future outcomes can detract from individuals' focus and concentration, leading to decreased efficiency and performance. Additionally, overthinking can foster a perfectionist mindset, wherein individuals set unrealistically high standards for themselves and become overly critical of their work.

In team settings, overthinking can manifest in communication breakdowns and conflict as individuals struggle to express their thoughts and ideas effectively. Misinterpretation of others' intentions or over-analysis of feedback can lead to misunderstandings and interpersonal tension, undermining collaboration and teamwork.

Overthinking in Personal Development

In the realm of personal development, overthinking can

impede individuals' growth and self-improvement efforts, leading to feelings of stagnation and frustration. One common manifestation of overthinking in personal development is analysis paralysis, wherein individuals become overwhelmed by the multitude of options and possibilities for self-improvement. Instead of taking action, they may become stuck in a perpetual cycle of planning and preparation, fearing making the wrong choice or failing to meet their goals.

Moreover, overthinking can foster a fixed mindset, wherein individuals believe that their abilities and intelligence are static and immutable. This mindset can hinder individuals' willingness to take risks or embrace challenges, as they fear failure or criticism. Instead of seeing setbacks as opportunities for growth, they may interpret them as evidence of their inherent inadequacy or incompetence.

Additionally, overthinking can lead to comparison and self-doubt as individuals measure their progress and success against external standards or benchmarks. Constantly comparing oneself to others or seeking validation from external sources can undermine individuals' self-confidence and self-worth, leading to feelings of inadequacy or unworthiness.

Conclusion

In conclusion, overthinking can manifest in various aspects of individuals' lives, including their relationships, work, and personal development. Whether through incessant rumination and insecurity in relationships, analysis paralysis and perfectionism in the workplace, or stagnation and self-doubt in personal development, overthinking can significantly impact individuals' well-being and success.

By recognizing the pervasive influence of overthinking and its detrimental effects, individuals can begin to take steps to cultivate healthier thinking habits and mitigate its impact on their lives. Through mindfulness, cognitive restructuring, and self-compassion, individuals can learn to challenge maladaptive thinking patterns and embrace a more balanced and resilient approach to life. By fostering self-awareness and developing effective coping strategies, individuals can navigate the challenges of overthinking and cultivate greater fulfillment and success in their relationships, work, and personal development journeys.

CHAPTER THREE

3.1 The Mind-Body Connection

Introduction

Chapter 3 of our exploration delves into the profound interconnection between the mind and body, emphasizing the crucial role this relationship plays in our overall well-being. Understanding the intricate dynamics of the mind-body connection is essential for fostering holistic health and resilience. In this chapter, we will explore how our thoughts and emotions influence our physical health and vice versa, and we will discuss practical strategies for harnessing this connection to promote vitality and balance.

Understanding the Mind-Body Connection

The mind-body connection refers to the intricate relationship between our thoughts, emotions, beliefs, and physical health. Research in fields such as psychoneuroimmunology has shed light on how our mental and emotional states impact our physiological functioning. For example, chronic stress has been linked to a range of health problems, including cardiovascular disease, immune dysfunction, and gastrointestinal disorders.

Similarly, our physical health can influence our mental and emotional well-being. For instance, chronic pain or illness can take a toll on our mood and outlook, leading to feelings of frustration, anxiety, or depression. Conversely, engaging in activities that promote physical health, such as exercise or mindfulness practices, can have a positive impact on our mental and emotional state, fostering a sense of well-being and resilience.

The Role of Stress Hormones

One of the key mechanisms through which the mind-body connection operates is the release of stress hormones, such as cortisol and adrenaline, in response to perceived threats or challenges. While these hormones are essential for mobilizing our body's resources to deal with stressors, chronic activation of the stress response can have detrimental effects on our health.

Prolonged exposure to elevated levels of stress hormones can disrupt our immune system, impair our cognitive function, and increase our risk of developing chronic health conditions such as hypertension, diabetes, and depression. Moreover, chronic stress has been implicated in the development and progression of inflammatory disorders, autoimmune diseases, and gastrointestinal problems.

The Impact of Mindfulness and Meditation

Mindfulness and meditation practices have gained increasing attention for their ability to promote physical health and psychological well-being by cultivating awareness and presence in the moment. Mindfulness involves paying attention to our thoughts, emotions, and bodily sensations without judgment, while meditation involves training the mind to focus and sustain attention.

Numerous studies have demonstrated the beneficial effects of mindfulness and meditation on stress reduction, immune function, and inflammatory markers. By practicing mindfulness and meditation regularly, individuals can lower their levels of stress hormones, reduce inflammation, and enhance their overall resilience to stress.

The Gut-Brain Axis

Another fascinating aspect of the mind-body connection is the gut-brain axis, a bidirectional communication network between the gastrointestinal tract and the central nervous system. Emerging research suggests that the health of our gut microbiota, the trillions of bacteria that inhabit our digestive system, can influence our mood, behavior, and cognitive function.

Disruptions in the gut-brain axis have been implicated in the development of mood disorders such as anxiety and depression, as well as neurological conditions such as Alzheimer's disease and Parkinson's disease. Conversely, interventions that promote gut health, such as probiotics, prebiotics, and dietary changes, have been shown to have a positive impact on mental and emotional well-being.

Practical Strategies for Nurturing the Mind-Body Connection

Mindful Eating: Paying attention to the sensory experience of eating, such as the taste, texture, and aroma of food, can enhance our enjoyment and satisfaction with meals. Mindful eating involves tuning into our body's hunger and fullness cues, eating slowly, and savoring each bite.

Physical Activity: Regular exercise has been shown to have numerous physical and mental health benefits, including reducing stress, improving mood, and enhancing cognitive function. Finding activities that you enjoy and incorporating them into your daily routine can help promote overall well-being.

Stress Management Techniques: Practicing relaxation techniques such as deep breathing, progressive muscle relaxation, and guided imagery can help lower stress hormone levels and promote a sense of calm and relaxation. Additionally, engaging in activities that bring you joy and fulfillment, such as spending time in nature, pursuing hobbies, or connecting with loved ones, can help counteract the negative effects of stress.

Sleep Hygiene: Prioritizing adequate sleep is essential for maintaining optimal physical and mental health. Establishing a regular sleep schedule, creating a restful sleep environment, and practicing relaxation techniques before bedtime can help improve sleep quality and promote overall well-being.

Social Connection: Cultivating meaningful connections with others is essential for our emotional and psychological well-being. Spending time with friends and family, participating in group activities or support groups, and volunteering or helping others can help foster a sense of belonging and social support.

Nutrition and Hydration: Eating a balanced diet rich in fruits, vegetables, whole grains, and lean proteins can provide essential nutrients that support physical and mental health. Staying hydrated by drinking plenty of water throughout the day is also important for maintaining optimal hydration and supporting bodily functions.

Mindfulness and Meditation Practices: Incorporating mindfulness and meditation practices into your daily routine can help cultivate awareness, presence, and resilience in the face of stress and adversity. Whether through formal meditation sessions or informal mindfulness practices such as mindful breathing or body scans, taking time to nourish your mind and spirit can have profound benefits for your overall well-being.

Conclusion

In conclusion, the mind-body connection plays a fundamental role in shaping our physical health, emotional well-being, and overall quality of life. By understanding how our thoughts, emotions, and behaviors influence our physiological functioning, we can cultivate greater awareness and agency in promoting holistic health and resilience. Through practices such as mindfulness, meditation, stress management, and nurturing social connections, we can harness the power of the mind-body connection to foster vitality, balance, and well-being in our lives.

3.2 Exploring the Physical Toll of Overthinking

Introduction

Overthinking, characterized by repetitive and intrusive thoughts, can take a significant toll not only on our mental well-being but also on our physical health. In this exploration, we delve into the various ways in which overthinking manifests physically, impacting different systems of the body. Understanding the physical consequences of overthinking is crucial for recognizing the importance of managing our thought patterns and adopting strategies to mitigate its harmful effects.

Impact on the Nervous System

Overthinking triggers the body's stress response, leading to the release of stress hormones such as cortisol and adrenaline. Prolonged activation of the stress response can have detrimental effects on the nervous system, contributing to symptoms such as headaches, migraines, and tension in the muscles.

Chronic overthinking can also disrupt the balance of neurotransmitters in the brain, leading to imbalances that contribute to mood disorders such as anxiety and depression. Additionally, overstimulation of the sympathetic nervous system, which is responsible for the body's fight-or-flight response, can lead to feelings of agitation, restlessness, and difficulty concentrating.

Impact on the Cardiovascular System

The physical toll of overthinking extends to the cardiovascular system, with chronic stress contributing to an increased risk of heart disease, hypertension, and other cardiovascular conditions. The release of stress hormones such as cortisol and adrenaline can elevate blood pressure and heart rate, placing strain on the heart and blood vessels over time.

Moreover, overthinking can contribute to unhealthy lifestyle habits such as poor diet, lack of exercise, and smoking, which further increase the risk of cardiovascular disease. Chronic stress has also been linked to the development and progression of atherosclerosis, the buildup of plaque in the arteries, which can lead to heart attacks and strokes.

Impact on the Immune System

The immune system is highly sensitive to the effects of stress, with chronic overthinking weakening the body's defenses and making it more susceptible to infections and illness. Prolonged activation of the stress response suppresses the immune system's ability to mount an effective defense against pathogens, leaving the body vulnerable to bacterial and viral infections.

Moreover, chronic stress can exacerbate inflammatory processes in the body, contributing to the development and progression of autoimmune diseases such as rheumatoid arthritis, lupus, and inflammatory bowel disease. Inflammation is also implicated in the pathogenesis of chronic conditions such as diabetes, obesity, and cancer, highlighting the far-reaching impact of overthinking on immune function and overall health.

Impact on Digestive Health

The digestive system is particularly sensitive to the effects of stress, with overthinking contributing to a range of gastrointestinal symptoms such as indigestion, acid reflux, and irritable bowel syndrome (IBS). Chronic stress can disrupt the balance of beneficial bacteria in the gut, leading to dysbiosis and impairing digestion and nutrient absorption.

Moreover, overthinking can exacerbate symptoms of functional gastrointestinal disorders such as IBS, with stress triggering flare-ups of abdominal pain, bloating, and diarrhea. The gut-brain axis, a bidirectional communication network between the gut and the brain, plays a crucial role in regulating digestion, mood, and stress response, highlighting the intimate connection between our mental and digestive health.

Impact on Sleep Patterns

Overthinking can disrupt sleep patterns, contributing to insomnia, sleep disturbances, and poor sleep quality. The constant barrage of intrusive thoughts and worries can make it difficult to relax and unwind at night, leading to difficulty falling asleep and staying asleep.

Moreover, overthinking can trigger physiological arousal and hyperarousal, making it challenging for the body and mind to transition into a state of restful sleep. Chronic sleep deprivation can have a host of negative consequences, including impaired cognitive function, mood disturbances, and increased risk of chronic health conditions such as obesity, diabetes, and cardiovascular disease.

Impact on Hormonal Balance

Chronic overthinking can disrupt the delicate balance of hormones in the body, contributing to hormonal imbalances that impact mood, energy levels, and overall well-being. The release of stress hormones such as cortisol and adrenaline can dysregulate the hypothalamic-pituitary-adrenal (HPA) axis, the body's primary stress response system, leading to imbalances in other hormones such as insulin, thyroid hormones, and reproductive hormones.

Moreover, overthinking can exacerbate symptoms of hormonal conditions such as polycystic ovary syndrome (PCOS), adrenal fatigue, and thyroid disorders. Hormonal imbalances can have far-reaching effects on various systems of the body, contributing to symptoms such as fatigue, weight gain, mood swings, and reproductive issues.

Conclusion

In conclusion, overthinking can take a significant toll on our physical health, contributing to a range of symptoms and conditions that impact different systems of the body. From the nervous system to the cardiovascular system, immune system, digestive health, sleep patterns, and hormonal balance, chronic overthinking has far-reaching effects that can compromise our overall well-being.

Recognizing the physical consequences of overthinking underscores the importance of managing our thought patterns and adopting strategies to promote relaxation, stress reduction, and emotional resilience. By cultivating mindfulness, practicing relaxation techniques, and seeking support from mental health professionals, individuals can mitigate the physical toll of overthinking and foster greater health and vitality in their lives.

3.3 The Role of Stress Hormones and Their Effects on Health

Introduction

Stress hormones play a crucial role in the body's response to perceived threats or challenges, triggering a cascade of physiological changes designed to help us cope with stressful situations. However, chronic activation of the stress response can have detrimental effects on our health and well-being. In this exploration, we delve into the role of stress hormones such as cortisol and adrenaline, their effects on various systems of the body, and strategies for managing stress to promote optimal health.

Understanding Stress Hormones

Stress hormones are chemical messengers produced by the body in response to stressors, whether physical, emotional, or psychological. The primary stress hormones involved in the body's stress response are cortisol and adrenaline (also known as epinephrine). These hormones are released by the adrenal glands, small glands located on top of the kidneys, in response to signals from the brain's hypothalamus and pituitary gland.

Cortisol, often referred to as the "stress hormone," plays a central role in the body's stress response. It helps regulate a wide range of physiological processes, including metabolism, immune function, inflammation, and the sleep-wake cycle. Adrenaline, on the other hand, is responsible for the immediate "fight-or-flight" response, mobilizing the body's resources to deal with acute stressors.

The Fight-or-Flight Response

When we encounter a perceived threat or danger, whether real or imagined, the body initiates the fight-or-flight response. This evolutionary survival mechanism is designed to help us respond quickly to potential threats by either confronting them (fight) or fleeing from them (flight).

During the fight-or-flight response, the brain sends signals to the adrenal glands to release adrenaline into the bloodstream. Adrenaline triggers a rapid increase in heart rate, blood pressure, and respiratory rate, preparing the body for action. It also dilates the pupils, increases blood flow to the muscles, and releases glucose into the bloodstream to provide energy for physical exertion. Additionally, cortisol levels rise in response to stress, helping to mobilize energy stores and suppress non-essential functions such as digestion and reproduction. Cortisol also plays a role in modulating the immune response and reducing inflammation, which can be beneficial in the short term but detrimental if prolonged.

Effects of Chronic Stress Hormone Activation

While the stress response is adaptive in the short term, chronic activation of stress hormones can have detrimental effects on health and well-being. Prolonged exposure to elevated levels of cortisol and adrenaline is associated with a range of negative consequences, including:

Cardiovascular Effects: Chronic stress hormone activation can contribute to hypertension, or high blood pressure, by increasing heart rate and constricting blood vessels. Over time, this can lead to damage to the blood vessels and an increased risk of heart disease, heart attack, and stroke.

Immune Suppression: Cortisol has immunosuppressive effects, meaning it suppresses the activity of the immune system. Prolonged exposure to high levels of cortisol can weaken the body's defenses against infections and make individuals more susceptible to illness.

Metabolic Effects: Cortisol plays a key role in regulating metabolism and blood sugar levels. Chronic stress hormone activation can lead to insulin resistance, where cells become less responsive to insulin, increasing the risk of type 2 diabetes. It can also contribute to weight gain, particularly around the abdomen, due to increased appetite and fat storage.

Digestive Disturbances: Chronic stress can disrupt normal digestive processes, leading to symptoms such as indigestion, acid reflux, and irritable bowel syndrome

(IBS). Cortisol inhibits digestion and nutrient absorption, while adrenaline can stimulate bowel movements and contribute to diarrhea.

Mood Disorders: Chronic stress hormone activation is associated with an increased risk of mood disorders such as anxiety and depression. High levels of cortisol can affect neurotransmitter levels in the brain, leading to imbalances that contribute to mood disturbances and emotional dysregulation.

Sleep Disturbances: Cortisol levels naturally fluctuate throughout the day, peaking in the morning to help us wake up and declining in the evening to promote sleep. However, chronic stress can disrupt this natural rhythm, leading to difficulty falling asleep, staying asleep, or achieving restorative sleep.

Managing Stress Hormones for Optimal Health

Given the detrimental effects of chronic stress hormone activation on health and well-being, it is essential to adopt strategies for managing stress effectively. Here are some evidence-based approaches for promoting stress resilience and optimizing health:

Stress Reduction Techniques: Practice relaxation techniques such as deep breathing, progressive muscle relaxation, and guided imagery to promote a state of calm and relaxation. Mindfulness meditation and yoga have also been shown to be effective in reducing stress hormone levels and promoting emotional well-being.

Regular Exercise: Engage in regular physical activity, such as walking, jogging, cycling, or swimming, to help reduce stress hormone levels and promote overall health. Exercise stimulates the release of endorphins, the body's natural feel-good chemicals, which can help improve mood and reduce anxiety.

Healthy Lifestyle Habits: Maintain a healthy lifestyle by eating a balanced diet, getting adequate sleep, and avoiding excessive alcohol, caffeine, and nicotine. Prioritize self-care activities such as spending time in nature, practicing hobbies, and connecting with loved ones.

Social Support: Cultivate strong social connections and seek support from friends, family, or support groups during times of stress. Sharing your feelings and experiences with others can provide emotional validation and perspective, reducing feelings of isolation and loneliness.

Cognitive Behavioral Techniques: Use cognitive behavioral techniques such as cognitive restructuring and problem-solving to challenge negative thought patterns and develop more adaptive coping strategies. Learning to reframe stressful situations in a more positive light can help reduce the impact of stress on physical and emotional well-being.

Mind-Body Practices: Explore mind-body practices such as tai chi, qigong, or biofeedback to promote relaxation, stress reduction, and mind-body awareness. These practices can help enhance resilience to stress and promote a sense of balance and harmony in daily life.

Conclusion

In conclusion, stress hormones play a vital role in the body's response to stress, mobilizing resources to help us cope with perceived threats or challenges. However, chronic activation of stress hormones can have detrimental effects on health and well-being, contributing to a range of physical and mental health problems.

By adopting strategies for managing stress effectively, such as relaxation techniques, regular exercise, healthy lifestyle habits, social support, cognitive behavioral techniques, and mind-body practices, individuals can promote stress resilience and optimize their overall health and well-being. Recognizing the role of stress hormones in health underscores the importance of taking proactive steps to reduce stress and cultivate a balanced and harmonious life.

3.4 Techniques for Managing Stress and Promoting Relaxation

Introduction

In today's fast-paced world, stress has become an inevitable part of life, impacting our physical health, mental well-being, and overall quality of life. However, it's essential to recognize that stress is manageable, and there are numerous effective techniques for promoting relaxation and resilience in the face of life's challenges. In this exploration, we delve into evidence-based strategies for managing stress and fostering a sense of calm and relaxation in daily life.

Deep Breathing Exercises

Deep breathing exercises are a simple yet powerful technique for promoting relaxation and reducing stress. By focusing on slow, deep breaths, you can activate the body's relaxation response and calm the nervous system. One effective deep breathing exercise is diaphragmatic breathing, also known as belly breathing. To practice diaphragmatic breathing, follow these steps:

1. Find a comfortable seated position and place one hand on your abdomen, just below your ribcage.
2. Inhale deeply through your nose, allowing your abdomen to rise as you fill your lungs with air.
3. Exhale slowly and completely through your mouth, feeling your abdomen fall as you release your breath.
4. Continue this deep breathing pattern for several minutes, focusing on the sensation of the breath moving in and out of your body.

Progressive Muscle Relaxation (PMR)

Progressive muscle relaxation is a technique that involves tensing and then relaxing different muscle groups in the body to promote physical and mental relaxation. PMR can help reduce muscle tension, lower blood pressure, and alleviate symptoms of stress and anxiety. To practice progressive muscle relaxation, follow these steps:

1. Find a quiet, comfortable space and sit or lie down in a relaxed position.
2. Starting with your feet, tense the muscles in your toes and hold for a few seconds, then release and relax

completely.

3. Move up to your calves, thighs, buttocks, abdomen, chest, arms, shoulders, neck, and face, tensing and relaxing each muscle group in turn.

4. As you tense each muscle group, focus on the sensations of tension and release, allowing yourself to let go of stress and tension with each exhalation.

Progressive Muscle Relaxation (PMR)

Progressive muscle relaxation is a technique that involves tensing and then relaxing different muscle groups in the body to promote physical and mental relaxation. PMR can help reduce muscle tension, lower blood pressure, and alleviate symptoms of stress and anxiety. To practice progressive muscle relaxation, follow these steps:

1. Find a quiet, comfortable space and sit in a relaxed, upright posture.

2. Close your eyes or gaze softly at a fixed point in front of you.

3. Bring your attention to the sensations of your breath as it moves in and out of your body.

4. Notice the rise and fall of your abdomen or the sensation of air passing through your nostrils.

5. When your mind wanders, gently bring your attention back to the breath without judgment or frustration.

6. Continue this practice for several minutes, allowing yourself to be fully present in each moment.

Visualization and Guided Imagery

Visualization and guided imagery are techniques that

involve mentally picturing a peaceful, calming scene or scenario to promote relaxation and reduce stress. Visualization can help distract the mind from stressful thoughts and evoke feelings of calm and tranquility. To practice visualization and guided imagery, follow these steps:

1. Find a comfortable seated position and close your eyes.
2. Take a few deep breaths to relax your body and calm your mind.
3. Picture yourself in a serene, peaceful setting, such as a sunny beach, lush forest, or quiet mountain retreat.
4. Use all of your senses to imagine the sights, sounds, smells, and sensations of this peaceful place.
5. Allow yourself to immerse fully in the experience, letting go of stress and tension with each breath.

Yoga and Tai Chi

Yoga and tai chi are ancient mind-body practices that combine gentle movements, deep breathing, and meditation to promote relaxation and well-being. Both yoga and tai chi have been shown to reduce stress, improve flexibility and balance, and enhance overall physical and mental health. To practice yoga or tai chi, consider attending a class led by a qualified instructor or following along with instructional videos or online tutorials.

Engaging in Creative Activities

Engaging in creative activities such as painting, drawing, writing, or crafting can be an effective way to promote relaxation and reduce stress. Creative activities allow you to express yourself freely, channeling your thoughts and emotions into a tangible form. Whether you're painting a picture, writing in a journal, or knitting a scarf, creative activities can provide a sense of focus, purpose, and accomplishment, helping to alleviate symptoms of stress and anxiety.

Spending Time in Nature

Spending time in nature is a natural antidote to stress, providing an opportunity to disconnect from the pressures of daily life and reconnect with the natural world. Whether you take a leisurely walk in the park, hike in the mountains, or simply sit and enjoy the sights and sounds of nature, spending time outdoors can promote relaxation, reduce stress hormone levels, and improve mood and well-being.

Conclusion

In conclusion, managing stress and promoting relaxation are essential for maintaining optimal physical and mental health in today's fast-paced world. By incorporating techniques such as deep breathing exercises, progressive muscle relaxation, mindfulness meditation, visualization and guided imagery, yoga and tai chi, engaging in creative activities, and spending time in nature, you can cultivate a sense of calm and resilience in the face of life's challenges. Experiment with different techniques to find what works best for you, and make relaxation a priority in your daily routine. By taking proactive steps to manage stress, you can enhance your overall quality of life and promote a greater sense of well-being.

CHAPTER FOUR

1. Cognitive Behavioral Strategies for Stress Management and Well-Being

Introduction

Chapter 4 delves into the realm of cognitive behavioral strategies, a powerful set of techniques for managing stress, fostering resilience, and promoting overall well-being. Rooted in the principles of cognitive psychology, cognitive behavioral strategies emphasize the interplay between thoughts, emotions, and behaviors, empowering individuals to challenge negative thinking patterns and develop healthier coping mechanisms. In this exploration, we delve into various cognitive behavioral strategies and their applications in managing stress and enhancing psychological resilience.

Understanding Cognitive Behavioral Therapy (CBT)

Cognitive behavioral therapy (CBT) is a widely practiced form of psychotherapy that focuses on identifying and challenging negative thought patterns and beliefs that contribute to emotional distress and maladaptive behaviors. CBT is based on the premise that our thoughts, emotions, and behaviors are interconnected and that changing our thoughts can lead to changes in our emotions and behaviors. In CBT, individuals work collaboratively with a therapist to identify and evaluate their automatic thoughts, cognitive distortions, and core beliefs. Through various techniques such as cognitive restructuring, behavioral experiments, and skills training, individuals learn to develop more adaptive ways of thinking and responding to stressors.

Cognitive Restructuring

Cognitive restructuring is a core technique in CBT that involves identifying and challenging negative or irrational thoughts and replacing them with more balanced and realistic ones. The goal of cognitive restructuring is to help individuals develop a more accurate and adaptive perspective on themselves, others, and the world around them.

One common cognitive distortion addressed in cognitive restructuring is "catastrophizing," wherein individuals exaggerate the negative consequences of a situation and imagine the worst possible outcome. Through cognitive restructuring, individuals learn to challenge catastrophic thoughts by examining the evidence for and against them, considering alternative explanations, and generating more balanced interpretations.

Behavioral Activation

Behavioral activation is another key component of CBT that focuses on increasing engagement in pleasurable and meaningful activities as a way to alleviate symptoms of depression and enhance mood. The premise of behavioral activation is that behaviors and emotions are interconnected, and that by increasing participation in rewarding activities, individuals can improve their mood and sense of well-being.

In behavioral activation, individuals work with their therapist to identify activities that bring them pleasure, satisfaction, and a sense of accomplishment. These activities may include hobbies, socializing with friends and family, exercising, or engaging in creative pursuits. By scheduling and prioritizing these activities in their daily routine, individuals can counteract feelings of depression and increase their overall level of functioning.

Stress Inoculation Training (SIT)

Stress inoculation training (SIT) is a cognitive behavioral technique that involves teaching individuals adaptive coping skills to manage stress and adversity. The goal of SIT is to help individuals develop a repertoire of coping strategies that they can draw upon when faced with challenging situations.

In SIT, individuals learn various coping skills such as relaxation techniques, assertiveness training, problem-solving skills, and cognitive restructuring. Through rehearsal and practice, individuals become better equipped to cope with stressors effectively and maintain a sense of control and mastery in their lives.

Mindfulness-Based Cognitive Therapy (MBCT)

Mindfulness-based cognitive therapy (MBCT) combines elements of cognitive therapy with mindfulness meditation practices to prevent relapse in individuals with recurrent depression. MBCT helps individuals become more aware of their thoughts, emotions, and bodily sensations without judgment, allowing them to break free from automatic patterns of thinking and responding.

In MBCT, individuals learn mindfulness meditation techniques such as mindful breathing, body scans, and mindful movement. By practicing mindfulness regularly, individuals develop greater self-awareness and emotional regulation skills, enabling them to respond to stressors with greater flexibility and resilience.

Problem-Solving Skills Training

Problem-solving skills training is a cognitive behavioral technique that teaches individuals systematic problem-solving techniques to address and resolve life's challenges effectively. The problem-solving process involves several steps, including identifying the problem, generating possible solutions, evaluating the pros and cons of each solution, selecting the best course of action, and implementing and evaluating the solution.

By learning problem-solving skills, individuals can approach stressful situations with a more structured and proactive mindset, reducing feelings of helplessness and increasing their sense of efficacy and control.

Application of Cognitive Behavioral Strategies in Daily Life

The principles and techniques of cognitive behavioral therapy can be applied in various areas of daily life to promote stress management and psychological resilience. Whether dealing with work-related stress, interpersonal conflicts, or health challenges, individuals can benefit from adopting cognitive behavioral strategies to navigate life's ups and downs more effectively.

For example, when faced with a challenging situation at work, individuals can use cognitive restructuring techniques to challenge negative thoughts and reframe the situation in a more positive light. They can also apply problem-solving skills to identify practical solutions and take proactive steps to address the issue.

In interpersonal relationships, individuals can use assertiveness training to communicate their needs and boundaries effectively, assertively expressing their thoughts and feelings while respecting the rights of others. They can also use mindfulness techniques to cultivate empathy, compassion, and emotional regulation, fostering healthier and more fulfilling relationships.

Conclusion

In conclusion, cognitive behavioral strategies offer powerful tools for managing stress, enhancing resilience, and promoting overall well-being. By challenging negative thought patterns, developing adaptive coping skills, and fostering greater self-awareness and emotional regulation, individuals can navigate life's challenges more effectively and thrive in the face of adversity. Whether through cognitive restructuring, behavioral activation, stress inoculation training, mindfulness-based cognitive therapy, problem-solving skills training, or other techniques, the principles of cognitive behavioral therapy can empower individuals to take control of their thoughts, emotions, and behaviors, leading to greater psychological health and fulfillment.

2. Introduction to Cognitive Behavioral Therapy (CBT) Techniques

Introduction

Cognitive Behavioral Therapy (CBT) is a widely practiced and evidence-based form of psychotherapy that focuses on addressing the interplay between thoughts, emotions, and behaviors. Developed in the 1960s by Dr. Aaron T. Beck, CBT is grounded in the belief that our thoughts influence our feelings and behaviors and that changing negative or maladaptive thought patterns can lead to improvements in emotional well-being and functioning. In this exploration, we will provide an introduction to the fundamental principles and techniques of CBT, highlighting its effectiveness in treating various mental health conditions and promoting overall psychological resilience.

Understanding the Cognitive Model

The cognitive model, upon which CBT is based, posits that our thoughts, beliefs, and interpretations of events shape our emotional responses and behavioral reactions.

According to this model, individuals' perceptions of themselves, others, and the world around them are filtered through cognitive schemas or frameworks, which influence their interpretations and judgments.

When individuals hold negative or distorted beliefs about themselves, others, or the future, they are more likely to experience negative emotions such as anxiety, depression, or anger. These negative emotions, in turn, can lead to maladaptive behaviors such as avoidance, withdrawal, or aggression, perpetuating a cycle of distress and dysfunction.

Core Principles of CBT

CBT is guided by several core principles that underpin its therapeutic approach:

Collaborative and Empathic Relationship: CBT is conducted in a collaborative and empathic manner, with the therapist and client working together as partners in the therapeutic process. The therapist provides support, validation, and guidance, helping the client develop insight into their thoughts, emotions, and behaviors.

Focus on the Present: CBT emphasizes the importance of focusing on the present moment and addressing current problems and challenges. While past experiences and traumas may be relevant to understanding current difficulties, the primary focus of CBT is on identifying and changing current patterns of thinking and behavior.

Problem-Solving Orientation: CBT is problem-focused and

goal-oriented, with an emphasis on identifying specific problems or symptoms and developing practical strategies for addressing them. The therapist and client work together to set clear, achievable goals for therapy and develop a structured plan for achieving them.

Education and Skill-Building: CBT provides education about the nature of psychological problems and teaches clients practical skills and techniques for managing their symptoms and improving their coping abilities. Clients learn to identify and challenge negative thought patterns, regulate their emotions, and develop healthier ways of thinking and behaving.

Structured and Time-Limited: CBT is structured and time-limited, typically consisting of a set number of sessions focused on specific treatment goals. Sessions are structured around an agenda, with the therapist and client collaboratively reviewing progress, discussing homework assignments, and planning for future sessions.

Common Techniques Used in CBT

CBT employs a variety of techniques and strategies to help individuals identify and challenge negative thought patterns, regulate their emotions, and change maladaptive behaviors. Some of the most commonly used techniques in CBT include:

Cognitive Restructuring: Cognitive restructuring involves identifying and challenging negative or irrational thoughts and replacing them with more balanced and realistic ones. This technique helps individuals develop a more accurate and adaptive perspective on themselves, others, and the world around them.

Behavioral Activation: Behavioral activation is a technique that focuses on increasing engagement in pleasurable and meaningful activities as a way to alleviate symptoms of depression and enhance mood. By scheduling and prioritizing enjoyable activities, individuals can counteract feelings of depression and increase their overall level of functioning.

Exposure Therapy: Exposure therapy is a technique used to treat anxiety disorders by gradually exposing individuals to feared situations or stimuli in a controlled and systematic manner. Through repeated exposure, individuals learn to confront their fears and develop coping skills to manage anxiety effectively.

Mindfulness and Relaxation Techniques: Mindfulness and relaxation techniques, such as mindful breathing, progressive muscle relaxation, and guided imagery, help individuals reduce stress and promote relaxation. These techniques cultivate awareness of the present moment and help individuals develop greater self-regulation and emotional resilience.

Problem-Solving Skills Training: Problem-solving skills training teaches individuals systematic problem-solving techniques to address and resolve life's challenges effectively. By breaking problems down into manageable steps and generating practical solutions, individuals can approach stressful situations with a more structured and proactive mindset.

Assertiveness Training: Assertiveness training helps individuals communicate their needs, preferences, and boundaries effectively, assertively expressing their thoughts and feelings while respecting the rights of others. This technique promotes healthy assertiveness and reduces feelings of resentment or frustration in interpersonal relationships.

Applications of CBT

CBT has been shown to be effective in treating a wide range of mental health conditions, including:

- Depression
- Anxiety disorders (e.g., generalized anxiety disorder, panic disorder, social anxiety disorder)
- Obsessive-compulsive disorder (OCD)
- Post-traumatic stress disorder (PTSD)
- Eating disorders (e.g., bulimia nervosa, binge-eating disorder)
- Substance use disorders
- Insomnia and other sleep disorders
- Chronic pain conditions
- Personality disorders (e.g., borderline personality disorder)

CBT is also used in various settings, including individual therapy, group therapy, couples therapy, and family therapy. It has been adapted for use with diverse populations, including children, adolescents, adults, older adults, and individuals from different cultural backgrounds.

Conclusion

In conclusion, cognitive behavioral therapy (CBT) is a highly effective and versatile approach to psychotherapy that addresses the interplay between thoughts, emotions, and behaviors. Grounded in the cognitive model, CBT helps individuals identify and challenge negative thought patterns, regulate their emotions, and develop healthier ways of thinking and behaving. By employing a variety of techniques and strategies, CBT can help individuals manage symptoms of depression, anxiety, and other mental health conditions, leading to improved well-being and functioning. As a structured, goal-oriented, and evidence-based approach, CBT offers hope and empowerment to individuals seeking relief from psychological distress and a path toward greater psychological resilience and fulfillment.

3. Challenging Cognitive Distortions: A Key Component of Cognitive Behavioral Therapy

Introduction

Cognitive distortions, also known as cognitive errors or thinking traps, are exaggerated or irrational thoughts that can contribute to feelings of anxiety, depression, and distress. Recognizing and challenging cognitive distortions is a central component of cognitive behavioral therapy (CBT), a widely practiced and evidence-based approach to psychotherapy. In this exploration, we delve into the nature of cognitive distortions, their impact on mental health, and effective strategies for challenging and reframing distorted thinking patterns.

Understanding Cognitive Distortions

Cognitive distortions are patterns of thinking characterized by inaccuracies, biases, and irrational beliefs about oneself, others, and the world. These distortions can lead to negative interpretations of events, heightened emotional reactions, and maladaptive behaviors. Common types of cognitive distortions include:

All-or-Nothing Thinking: Also known as black-and-white thinking, this distortion involves viewing situations in extreme, polarized terms with no middle ground or shades of gray. Individuals engage in all-or-nothing thinking when they perceive situations as either perfect or complete failure without acknowledging the nuances or complexities involved.

Catastrophizing: Catastrophizing involves magnifying or exaggerating the negative consequences of a situation and imagining the worst possible outcome. Individuals who engage in catastrophizing often anticipate disaster or assume that a minor setback will lead to a catastrophic chain of events.

Overgeneralization: Overgeneralization involves drawing broad conclusions based on limited evidence or single instances. Individuals who overgeneralize may use words like "always" or "never" to describe their experiences, assuming that a negative outcome in one situation will inevitably occur in all similar situations.

Mind Reading: Mind reading involves assuming that one knows what others are thinking or feeling without sufficient evidence. Individuals who engage in mind reading may interpret neutral or ambiguous cues as evidence of negative thoughts or intentions from others.

Personalization: Personalization involves attributing external events or circumstances to oneself, even when there is no logical connection. Individuals who personalize may blame themselves for events beyond their control or assume responsibility for the actions of others.

Discounting the Positive: Discounting the positive involves minimizing or disregarding positive experiences, accomplishments, or feedback. Individuals who discount the positive may dismiss compliments, achievements, or instances of success as insignificant or unworthy of attention.

Impact of Cognitive Distortions on Mental Health

Cognitive distortions can have a profound impact on mental health and well-being, contributing to symptoms of anxiety, depression, and other psychological disorders. When individuals consistently engage in distorted thinking patterns, they may experience:

Increased Anxiety: Cognitive distortions can fuel feelings of worry, uncertainty, and fear, leading to heightened anxiety and stress. Catastrophizing, in particular, can exacerbate feelings of anxiety by magnifying the perceived threat of potential dangers or negative outcomes.

Persistent Sadness: Cognitive distortions such as overgeneralization and all-or-nothing thinking can contribute to feelings of hopelessness, worthlessness, and despair. Individuals may become trapped in a cycle of negative thinking, perceiving themselves and their circumstances in excessively negative terms.

Low Self-Esteem: Cognitive distortions often involve negative beliefs about oneself, leading to feelings of inadequacy, self-doubt, and low self-esteem. Personalization and discounting the positive can undermine individuals' confidence and self-worth, perpetuating a cycle of self-criticism and self-sabotage.

Impaired Problem-Solving: Cognitive distortions can interfere with effective problem-solving and decision-making, as individuals may struggle to accurately assess situations and generate viable solutions. Overgeneralization and catastrophizing can lead to rigid thinking patterns and tunnel vision, making it difficult to consider alternative perspectives or courses of action.

Challenging Cognitive Distortions

Challenging cognitive distortions is a key goal of CBT, as it helps individuals develop more accurate and balanced ways of thinking about themselves, others, and the world. Several techniques and strategies are used in CBT to challenge cognitive distortions, including:

Identifying Cognitive Distortions: The first step in challenging cognitive distortions is to identify and recognize them when they occur. This involves developing awareness of common cognitive distortions and learning to identify them in one's own thinking patterns. Keeping a thought journal or diary can be helpful in tracking and analyzing distorted thoughts.

Reality Testing: Reality testing involves evaluating the evidence for and against a distorted thought or belief. Individuals are encouraged to examine the facts objectively, consider alternative explanations or interpretations, and assess the likelihood of different outcomes. By questioning the validity of distorted thoughts, individuals can gain perspective and reduce their impact on emotions and behavior.

Cognitive Restructuring: Cognitive restructuring involves actively challenging and changing distorted thoughts and beliefs through reasoned argument and evidence-based reasoning. This technique helps individuals develop more accurate and balanced ways of thinking by replacing distorted thoughts with more rational and realistic ones. Cognitive restructuring may involve asking questions such as:

- "What evidence supports this thought/belief?"
- "Is there any evidence against this thought/belief?"
- "What would a more balanced perspective look like?"
- "What are some alternative explanations for this situation?"

Behavioral Experiments: Behavioral experiments involve testing the validity of distorted thoughts through real-world experimentation and observation. Individuals are encouraged to conduct experiments to gather evidence for or against their distorted beliefs, allowing them to challenge and modify their thinking patterns based on the results. Behavioral experiments help individuals build confidence in their ability to cope with challenging situations and develop more adaptive ways of thinking and behaving.

Mindfulness and Acceptance: Mindfulness and acceptance techniques can help individuals develop a non-judgmental and compassionate attitude toward their thoughts and emotions. By practicing mindfulness meditation and mindfulness-based stress reduction (MBSR) techniques, individuals can learn to observe their thoughts without becoming entangled in them, allowing for greater clarity and perspective.

Gratitude and Positive Psychology: Gratitude exercises and positive psychology interventions can help counteract cognitive distortions by focusing attention on positive aspects of one's life and experiences. By cultivating gratitude and appreciation for the good things in life, individuals can shift their attention away from negative thoughts and emotions, leading to greater happiness and well-being.

Conclusion

In conclusion, cognitive distortions are common thinking errors that can contribute to feelings of anxiety, depression, and distress. Challenging cognitive distortions is a central focus of cognitive behavioral therapy (CBT), a highly effective and evidence-based approach to psychotherapy.

By identifying, evaluating, and reframing distorted thoughts and beliefs, individuals can develop more accurate and balanced ways of thinking, leading to improved mental health and well-being. Through techniques such as reality testing, cognitive restructuring, behavioral experiments, mindfulness, and gratitude, individuals can cultivate greater self-awareness, resilience, and emotional regulation, empowering them to live more fulfilling and satisfying lives.

4. Building Resilience Through Reframing and Positive Self-Talk

Introduction

Resilience, the ability to bounce back from adversity, is a crucial skill that empowers individuals to navigate life's challenges with strength and adaptability. Reframing and positive self-talk are powerful cognitive strategies that can help individuals build resilience by promoting a more optimistic and adaptive mindset. In this exploration, we delve into the concepts of reframing and positive self-talk, their role in fostering resilience, and practical techniques for incorporating these strategies into daily life.

Understanding Resilience

Resilience is often described as the capacity to withstand and recover from difficult experiences, adversity, or trauma. Resilient individuals possess inner strength, flexibility, and optimism, enabling them to cope effectively with stress, setbacks, and obstacles. While resilience is influenced by various factors, including genetics, personality traits, and life experiences, it is also a skill that can be cultivated and developed over time.

Reframing: Shifting Perspectives for Resilience

Reframing involves consciously changing the way we perceive and interpret situations, events, or challenges. Instead of viewing difficulties as insurmountable obstacles, individuals can reframe them as opportunities for growth, learning, and personal development. Reframing allows individuals to shift their perspective from one of victimhood or helplessness to one of empowerment and resilience. There are several techniques for reframing:

Cognitive Restructuring: Cognitive restructuring involves identifying and challenging negative or distorted thoughts and replacing them with more balanced and realistic ones. By examining the evidence for and against a particular interpretation of events, individuals can develop a more accurate and adaptive perspective. For example, instead of catastrophizing and assuming the worst possible outcome, individuals can challenge catastrophic thoughts by considering alternative explanations and focusing on their strengths and coping resources.

Finding Silver Linings: Finding silver linings involves searching for positive aspects or opportunities in the midst of adversity. Even in the face of challenges, there may be hidden blessings, lessons, or silver linings that can be uncovered with a shift in perspective. For example, a job loss may provide an opportunity for career exploration and growth, or a setback in a relationship may lead to greater self-awareness and personal insight.

Seeking Growth and Learning: Reframing challenges as opportunities for growth and learning can help individuals develop resilience and adaptability. Viewing difficulties as temporary setbacks or stepping stones on the path to success can foster a sense of optimism and perseverance. By reframing setbacks as valuable learning experiences, individuals can extract meaning and wisdom from adversity, enabling them to bounce back stronger and more resilient than before.

Positive Self-Talk: Harnessing the Power of Positive Thinking

Positive self-talk involves using affirming, encouraging, and supportive language to counteract negative thoughts and beliefs. By consciously choosing positive and empowering words and phrases, individuals can cultivate a more optimistic and resilient mindset. Positive self-talk serves as an internal dialogue that reinforces self-confidence, self-efficacy, and self-belief, empowering individuals to face challenges with courage and determination. There are several techniques for practicing positive self-talk:

Affirmations: Affirmations are positive statements or affirming beliefs that individuals repeat to themselves regularly. Affirmations can be tailored to specific goals, challenges, or areas of growth, reinforcing desired qualities or attributes. For example, affirmations such as "I am resilient," "I am capable of overcoming obstacles," or "I believe in myself" can help build confidence and self-esteem.

Replacing Negative Thoughts: Positive self-talk involves consciously replacing negative or self-defeating thoughts with more positive and empowering ones. When negative thoughts arise, individuals can challenge and reframe them by asking themselves:

- "Is this thought helpful or accurate?"
- "What evidence do I have to support this thought?"
- "What would I say to a friend in this situation?" By replacing negative thoughts with more balanced and compassionate ones, individuals can build resilience and self-confidence.

Visualization and Imagery: Visualization and imagery techniques involve mentally rehearsing positive outcomes and visualizing success. By picturing themselves overcoming challenges, achieving goals, and realizing their dreams, individuals can cultivate a sense of optimism and motivation. Visualization can help individuals build confidence and resilience by creating a mental blueprint for success.

Self-Compassion: Self-compassion involves treating oneself with kindness, understanding, and acceptance, especially in the face of setbacks or failures. Instead of engaging in self-criticism or self-blame, individuals practice self-compassion by offering themselves words of encouragement and support. Self-compassion allows individuals to acknowledge their humanity, imperfections, and limitations, fostering resilience and emotional well-being.

Practical Techniques for Building Resilience Through Reframing and Positive Self-Talk :

Journaling: Keeping a journal or gratitude journal can be a powerful tool for practicing reframing and positive self-talk. Writing down thoughts, feelings, and experiences allows individuals to reflect on their perspectives and identify opportunities for reframing. Additionally, writing down affirmations or positive statements can help reinforce positive self-talk and build resilience.

Mindfulness Meditation: Mindfulness meditation involves cultivating present-moment awareness and non-judgmental acceptance of thoughts and emotions. By practicing mindfulness, individuals can observe their thoughts without becoming entangled in them, allowing for greater clarity and perspective. Mindfulness meditation can help individuals develop resilience by promoting self-awareness, emotional regulation, and acceptance of change.

Social Support: Seeking support from friends, family, or support groups can provide valuable validation, encouragement, and perspective. Sharing experiences and challenges with others allows individuals to gain new insights, receive feedback, and feel less alone in their struggles. Social support fosters resilience by providing a sense of connection, belonging, and mutual support.

Self-Care: Practicing self-care activities such as exercise, healthy eating, adequate sleep, and relaxation techniques can promote resilience and well-being. Taking care of one's physical, emotional, and mental health strengthens the foundation for resilience and enhances coping abilities.

Engaging in activities that bring joy, pleasure, and fulfillment nourishes the body, mind, and spirit, fostering resilience and vitality.

Conclusion

In conclusion, reframing and positive self-talk are powerful cognitive strategies for building resilience and promoting psychological well-being. By consciously changing the way we perceive and interpret challenges, events, and setbacks, we can cultivate a more optimistic and adaptive mindset. Through techniques such as cognitive restructuring, finding silver linings, and seeking growth and learning, individuals can reframe adversity as opportunities for growth, learning, and personal development.

Additionally, by practicing positive self-talk techniques such as affirmations, replacing negative thoughts, visualization, and self-compassion, individuals can reinforce self-confidence, self-esteem, and self-belief, empowering them to face challenges with courage and resilience. By integrating reframing and positive self-talk into daily life, individuals can build the resilience needed to thrive in the face of adversity and emerge stronger and more resilient than before.

CHAPTER FIVE

1. Mindfulness and Meditation: Cultivating Presence and Resilience

Introduction

In today's fast-paced world, mindfulness and meditation have emerged as powerful practices for promoting mental health, emotional well-being, and resilience. Rooted in ancient contemplative traditions, mindfulness and meditation involve cultivating present-moment awareness, non-judgmental acceptance, and inner peace. In this chapter, we explore the principles and benefits of mindfulness and meditation, their applications in promoting resilience, and practical techniques for integrating these practices into daily life.

Understanding Mindfulness and Meditation

Mindfulness is the practice of intentionally bringing attention to the present moment with openness, curiosity, and acceptance. Mindfulness involves observing thoughts, emotions, sensations, and external stimuli without judgment or attachment. By cultivating mindfulness, individuals develop greater self-awareness, emotional regulation, and resilience in the face of life's challenges.

Meditation is a formal practice that cultivates mindfulness and concentration through techniques such as focused attention, open monitoring, and loving-kindness. Meditation involves training the mind to be present, calm, and centered, often through practices such as breath awareness, body scan, loving-kindness meditation, and mindful movement.

Benefits of Mindfulness and Meditation

Mindfulness and meditation offer a wide range of benefits for mental, emotional, and physical well-being. Some of the key benefits include:

Stress Reduction: Mindfulness and meditation have been shown to reduce stress levels by promoting relaxation, calming the nervous system, and lowering levels of stress hormones such as cortisol. By cultivating present-moment awareness and nonreactive acceptance, individuals can respond to stressors with greater resilience and equanimity.

Emotional Regulation: Mindfulness and meditation help individuals develop greater emotional awareness and regulation skills, enabling them to navigate difficult emotions such as anxiety, depression, anger, and sadness more effectively. By observing emotions without judgment or reactivity, individuals can cultivate a sense of inner peace and equanimity.

Improved Concentration and Focus: Meditation practices such as focused attention and concentration training help individuals strengthen their ability to sustain attention and focus on a single object or task. By training the mind to be present and centered, individuals can enhance cognitive function, productivity, and performance in various domains of life.

Enhanced Self-Awareness: Mindfulness and meditation foster greater self-awareness by helping individuals observe thoughts, emotions, and sensations with clarity and objectivity. By developing insight into the nature of the mind and its habitual patterns, individuals can make more conscious choices and respond to life's challenges with greater wisdom and discernment.

Increased Resilience: Mindfulness and meditation cultivate resilience by helping individuals develop a sense of inner strength, adaptability, and acceptance in the face of adversity. By learning to embrace uncertainty and change with openness and curiosity, individuals can bounce back from setbacks and setbacks more easily, emerging stronger and more resilient than before.

Practical Techniques for Cultivating Mindfulness and Meditation :

Breath Awareness Meditation: Breath awareness meditation involves focusing attention on the sensations of the breath as it moves in and out of the body. To practice breath awareness meditation, find a quiet, comfortable space and sit or lie down in a relaxed posture. Close your eyes and bring your attention to the natural rhythm of your breath, noticing the sensations of inhalation and exhalation. If the mind wanders, gently bring your attention back to the breath without judgment or frustration.

Body Scan Meditation: Body scan meditation involves systematically bringing attention to different parts of the body, from head to toe, and observing sensations without judgment. To practice body scan meditation, lie down in a comfortable position and bring your attention to the sensations in your body. Start at the top of your head and slowly move downward, noticing any areas of tension, discomfort, or relaxation. Allow yourself to fully experience each sensation, letting go of any tension or resistance with each exhalation.

Loving-Kindness Meditation: Loving-kindness meditation involves cultivating feelings of compassion, kindness, and goodwill toward oneself and others. To practice loving-kindness meditation, find a quiet, comfortable space and sit in a relaxed posture. Close your eyes and bring to mind someone you care about, such as a loved one, friend, or mentor. Repeat phrases such as "May you be happy, may you be healthy, may you be safe, may you be at ease" as you cultivate feelings of love and compassion.

Mindful Movement: Mindful movement practices such as yoga, tai chi, and qigong combine gentle movement with breath awareness and meditation techniques. These practices help individuals develop greater body awareness, flexibility, and relaxation, promoting physical and mental well-being. Whether through a formal class or self-guided practice, mindful movement can be a powerful way to cultivate mindfulness and meditation in daily life.

Daily Mindfulness Practices: Incorporating mindfulness into daily activities such as eating, walking, and listening can help individuals cultivate present-moment awareness and mindfulness in everyday life. By bringing attention to the sensory experience of each moment, individuals can savor the richness of life and find moments of peace and clarity amidst the busyness of daily life.

Applications of Mindfulness and Meditation in Promoting Resilience:

Stress Management: Mindfulness and meditation are effective tools for managing stress and promoting relaxation. By bringing attention to the present moment and observing thoughts and emotions with detachment, individuals can reduce reactivity and respond to stressors with greater equanimity.

Emotional Regulation: Mindfulness and meditation help individuals develop greater emotional awareness and regulation skills, enabling them to navigate difficult emotions such as anxiety, depression, and anger more effectively. By cultivating a non-judgmental attitude toward emotions and allowing them to arise and pass without clinging or aversion, individuals can develop greater emotional resilience and well-being.

Cognitive Flexibility: Mindfulness and meditation foster cognitive flexibility by helping individuals develop a more open and curious attitude toward their thoughts and beliefs. By observing thoughts without attachment or identification, individuals can challenge rigid thinking patterns and cultivate a more adaptive and resilient mindset.

Self-Compassion: Mindfulness and meditation cultivate self-compassion by encouraging individuals to treat themselves with kindness, understanding, and acceptance. By acknowledging and validating their own suffering with compassion and empathy, individuals can develop greater resilience and self-acceptance in the face of adversity.

Meaning-Making: Mindfulness and meditation help individuals find meaning and purpose in difficult experiences by cultivating a sense of inner peace, wisdom, and acceptance. By embracing life's challenges as opportunities for growth, learning, and transformation, individuals can develop greater resilience and well-being.

Conclusion

In conclusion, mindfulness and meditation are powerful practices for cultivating presence, resilience, and well-being. By bringing attention to the present moment with openness, curiosity, and acceptance, individuals can develop greater self-awareness, emotional regulation, and cognitive flexibility. Through techniques such as breath awareness, body scan, loving-kindness meditation, and mindful movement, individuals can cultivate mindfulness and meditation in daily life, promoting relaxation, stress reduction, and emotional well-being.

2. Understanding Mindfulness and Its Benefits for Overthinkers

Introduction

In today's fast-paced and information-saturated world, overthinking has become a common challenge for many individuals. Overthinkers often find themselves caught in a cycle of repetitive and unproductive thoughts, leading to increased stress, anxiety, and mental fatigue. Mindfulness, a practice rooted in ancient contemplative traditions, offers a powerful antidote to overthinking by cultivating present-moment awareness and non-judgmental acceptance. In this exploration, we delve into the concept of mindfulness, its benefits for overthinkers, and practical strategies for integrating mindfulness into daily life.

Understanding Mindfulness

Mindfulness is the practice of intentionally bringing attention to the present moment with openness, curiosity, and acceptance. Rooted in Buddhist contemplative traditions, mindfulness has been adapted into secular contexts and therapeutic interventions, such as Mindfulness-Based Stress Reduction (MBSR) and Mindfulness-Based Cognitive Therapy (MBCT). Mindfulness involves observing thoughts, emotions, sensations, and external stimuli without judgment or attachment, cultivating a sense of inner peace, clarity, and equanimity.

For overthinkers, mindfulness offers a way to break free from the cycle of rumination and worry by bringing attention back to the present moment. By observing thoughts without getting caught up in their content or meaning, overthinkers can develop greater self-awareness and emotional regulation skills, enabling them to respond to challenges with greater clarity and resilience.

Benefits of Mindfulness for Overthinkers:

Reduced Rumination: Overthinkers often get stuck in repetitive and unproductive thought patterns, leading to rumination and mental exhaustion. Mindfulness helps break the cycle of rumination by bringing attention back to the present moment, allowing overthinkers to let go of excessive worry and rumination about the past or future.

Increased Emotional Regulation: Overthinkers may struggle with intense emotions such as anxiety, stress, and overwhelm. Mindfulness helps overthinkers develop greater emotional regulation skills by allowing them to observe emotions with detachment and nonreactivity. By cultivating a sense of inner calm and equanimity, overthinkers can respond to emotions more skillfully and effectively.

Improved Decision-Making: Overthinking can impair decision-making by leading to indecision, analysis paralysis, and second-guessing. Mindfulness helps overthinkers make decisions more confidently and intuitively by cultivating clarity, focus, and perspective. By bringing attention to the present moment and observing thoughts without judgment, overthinkers can access their intuition and inner wisdom more readily.

Enhanced Cognitive Flexibility: Overthinkers may exhibit rigid thinking patterns and difficulty shifting perspectives. Mindfulness promotes cognitive flexibility by encouraging overthinkers to approach thoughts with curiosity and openness. By observing thoughts as passing phenomena rather than fixed truths, overthinkers can develop greater flexibility and adaptability in their thinking.

Stress Reduction: Overthinking is often accompanied by heightened levels of stress and anxiety. Mindfulness helps overthinkers reduce stress by promoting relaxation, calming the nervous system, and lowering levels of stress hormones such as cortisol. By cultivating present-moment awareness and nonreactive acceptance, overthinkers can respond to stressors with greater equanimity and resilience.

Practical Strategies for Integrating Mindfulness into Daily Life:

Mindful Breathing: Mindful breathing is a simple yet powerful technique for cultivating present-moment awareness and relaxation. To practice mindful breathing, find a quiet and comfortable space and bring attention to the sensations of the breath as it moves in and out of the body. Notice the rise and fall of the abdomen or the sensations of air passing through the nostrils. If the mind wanders, gently bring attention back to the breath without judgment or frustration.

Body Scan Meditation: Body scan meditation involves systematically bringing attention to different parts of the body, from head to toe, and observing sensations without judgment. To practice body scan meditation, lie down in a comfortable position and bring attention to each part of the body, starting with the feet and moving upward to the head. Notice any areas of tension, discomfort, or relaxation, allowing yourself to fully experience each sensation.

Mindful Walking: Mindful walking is a way to bring mindfulness into everyday activities such as walking. To practice mindful walking, focus attention on the sensations of the feet as they make contact with the ground, noticing the rhythm and pace of each step. Bring attention to the sights, sounds, and smells of the environment, allowing yourself to fully experience the present moment with curiosity and openness.

Mindful Eating: Mindful eating involves bringing awareness to the sensory experience of eating, such as the taste, texture, and aroma of food. To practice mindful eating, slow down and savor each bite, noticing the flavors and sensations in your mouth. Pay attention to the process of chewing and swallowing, and notice any thoughts or emotions that arise without judgment.

Daily Mindfulness Practice: Incorporating mindfulness into daily routines can help overthinkers cultivate present-moment awareness and mindfulness in everyday life. Set aside time each day for formal mindfulness practice, such as meditation or deep breathing exercises. Additionally, find opportunities throughout the day to bring attention to the present moment, such as during daily activities like showering, brushing teeth, or commuting.

Conclusion

In conclusion, mindfulness offers valuable benefits for overthinkers by promoting present-moment awareness, emotional regulation, and resilience. By cultivating mindfulness, overthinkers can reduce rumination, improve decision-making, and enhance overall well-being. Through practical strategies such as mindful breathing, body scan meditation, mindful walking, mindful eating, and daily mindfulness practice, overthinkers can integrate mindfulness into daily life and reap its transformative benefits. With consistent practice and commitment, overthinkers can develop greater clarity, calm, and equanimity, enabling them to navigate life's challenges with greater ease and resilience.

3. Practical Mindfulness Exercises for Everyday Life

Introduction

In our fast-paced and often hectic lives, finding moments of peace, clarity, and presence can be challenging. However, integrating mindfulness into our daily routines can help us cultivate a greater sense of awareness, calm, and well-being. Mindfulness involves paying attention to the present moment with openness, curiosity, and non-judgmental awareness. In this guide, we'll explore practical mindfulness exercises that can be easily incorporated into everyday life, helping you cultivate mindfulness and enhance your overall quality of life.

Mindful Breathing

One of the simplest and most accessible mindfulness exercises is mindful breathing. This exercise can be practiced anytime and anywhere, making it ideal for integrating into your daily routine. Here's how to practice mindful breathing:

- Find a comfortable position, either sitting or lying down, and close your eyes if it feels comfortable.
- Bring your attention to your breath, noticing the sensations of inhaling and exhaling.
- Focus on the rise and fall of your abdomen or the sensation of air passing through your nostrils.
- If your mind wanders, gently bring your attention back to your breath without judgment.
- Continue to breathe mindfully for a few minutes, gradually lengthening your inhalations and exhalations if they feel natural.

Practicing mindful breathing can help you calm your mind, reduce stress, and cultivate a greater sense of presence and relaxation in your daily life.

Body Scan Meditation

Body scan meditation is a practice that involves systematically bringing attention to different parts of the body, noticing sensations without judgment. This exercise can help you develop greater body awareness and release tension. Here's how to practice body scan meditation:

- Find a comfortable position, either sitting or lying down, and close your eyes if it feels comfortable.
- Begin by bringing your attention to your feet and noticing any sensations such as warmth, tingling, or pressure.
- Slowly move your attention upward through your body, paying attention to each part in turn, including your legs, hips, abdomen, chest, arms, hands, neck, and head.
- Notice any areas of tension or discomfort, and allow them to soften and release with each breath.
- If your mind wanders, gently bring your attention back to the sensations in your body without judgment.
- Continue to scan your body from head to toe, taking your time and breathing deeply.

Body scan meditation can help you develop greater relaxation, body awareness, and acceptance in your daily life.

Mindful Walking

Mindful walking is a practice that involves bringing awareness to each step you take, noticing the sensations of movement and the environment around you. This exercise can be practiced indoors or outdoors and is particularly effective for grounding and centering yourself. Here's how to practice mindful walking:

- Find a quiet and safe place to walk, either indoors or outdoors, where you can move freely without distractions.

- Begin by standing still and taking a few deep breaths, centering yourself in the present moment.
- As you start to walk, bring your attention to the sensations in your feet and legs, noticing the contact with the ground and the movement of your muscles.
- Pay attention to the rhythm and pace of your steps, allowing yourself to walk at a comfortable and natural speed.
- Notice the sights, sounds, and smells around you, bringing awareness to the present moment experience.
- If your mind wanders, gently bring your attention back to the sensations of walking without judgment.
- Continue to walk mindfully for a few minutes, allowing yourself to fully experience each step.

Mindful walking can help you connect with your body, quiet your mind, and find moments of peace and presence in your daily life.

Mindful Eating

Mindful eating is a practice that involves bringing awareness to the sensory experience of eating, including the taste, texture, and aroma of food. This exercise can help you cultivate a greater appreciation for food and develop a healthier relationship with eating. Here's how to practice mindful eating:

- Choose a meal or snack to eat mindfully, preferably one that you can eat slowly and without distractions.
- Before you begin eating, take a moment to pause and appreciate the food in front of you, noticing its colors,

textures, and smells.

- Take a few deep breaths to center yourself in the present moment.
- As you take your first bite, bring your attention to the taste and texture of the food, noticing how it feels in your mouth and on your tongue.
- Chew slowly and mindfully, paying attention to the sensations of chewing and swallowing.
- Notice any thoughts or emotions that arise as you eat, allowing them to pass without judgment.
- If your mind wanders, gently bring your attention back to the sensory experience of eating.

Mindful eating can help you develop greater awareness of hunger and fullness cues, savor your food more fully, and cultivate a healthier relationship with eating.

Daily Mindfulness Check-In

Finally, a simple yet effective mindfulness exercise is to incorporate daily mindfulness check-ins into your routine. This exercise involves taking a few moments throughout the day to pause, breathe, and bring awareness to your present-moment experience. Here's how to practice a daily mindfulness check-in:

- Set aside several times throughout the day to pause and check in with yourself, such as when you wake up, before meals, or before bed.
- Take a few deep breaths to center yourself in the present moment.

- Notice how you're feeling physically, emotionally, and mentally in that moment without judgment.
- Bring awareness to any thoughts, emotions, or sensations that are present for you, allowing them to simply be without trying to change or fix them.
- Take a moment to express gratitude for the opportunity to pause and connect with yourself

Daily mindfulness check-ins can help you develop greater self-awareness, presence, and resilience in your daily life.

Conclusion

In conclusion, mindfulness exercises offer practical and accessible ways to cultivate greater awareness, presence, and well-being in everyday life. By integrating mindfulness into your daily routine, you can reduce stress, increase relaxation, and develop greater resilience in the face of life's challenges. Whether you practice mindful breathing, body scan meditation, mindful walking, mindful eating, or daily mindfulness check-ins, finding moments of peace and presence can help you live more fully and authentically. Experiment with different mindfulness exercises to see which ones resonate most with you, and remember that consistency and patience are key to cultivating a mindfulness practice that enriches your life.

4. Incorporating Meditation into Your Routine to Quiet the Mind

Introduction

In the modern world, where our minds are constantly bombarded with information and stimuli, finding moments of peace and quiet can be a challenge. However, meditation offers a powerful tool for quieting the mind, reducing stress, and promoting overall well-being. By incorporating meditation into your daily routine, you can cultivate a sense of inner calm and clarity that can positively impact every aspect of your life. In this guide, we'll explore the benefits of meditation for quieting the mind and practical strategies for integrating meditation into your routine.

Understanding Meditation

Meditation is a practice that involves training the mind to focus attention and cultivate awareness. While there are many different forms of meditation, they all share a common goal of quieting the chatter of the mind and promoting a sense of inner peace and stillness. Some common types of meditation include mindfulness meditation, focused attention meditation, loving-kindness meditation, and transcendental meditation.

At its core, meditation involves bringing attention to the present moment with openness, curiosity, and non-judgmental awareness. By observing thoughts, emotions, sensations, and external stimuli without getting caught up in them, individuals can develop greater clarity, calm, and resilience in the face of life's challenges.

Benefits of Meditation for Quieting the Mind:

Reduced Mental Chatter: One of the primary benefits of meditation is its ability to quiet the incessant chatter of the mind. Through regular practice, individuals learn to observe thoughts as passing phenomena rather than fixed truths, allowing them to detach from the stream of mental commentary and experience greater peace and stillness.

Increased Focus and Concentration: Meditation helps individuals develop greater focus and concentration by training the mind to sustain attention on a single object or point of focus. By practicing meditation regularly, individuals can strengthen their attentional muscles and become less easily distracted by external stimuli.

Enhanced Emotional Regulation: Meditation promotes emotional regulation by helping individuals develop greater awareness and acceptance of their emotions. By observing emotions with detachment and nonreactivity, individuals can respond to them more skillfully and effectively, reducing emotional reactivity and increasing emotional resilience.

Stress Reduction: Meditation has been shown to reduce stress levels by promoting relaxation, calming the nervous system, and lowering levels of stress hormones such as cortisol. By cultivating present-moment awareness and nonreactive acceptance, individuals can respond to stressors with greater equanimity and resilience.

Improved Sleep Quality: Regular meditation practice has

been linked to improved sleep quality and reduced insomnia. By promoting relaxation and reducing stress levels, meditation can help individuals achieve a state of calm and tranquility that facilitates restful sleep.

Practical Strategies for Incorporating Meditation into Your Routine:

Start Small: If you're new to meditation, start with just a few minutes of practice each day and gradually increase the duration as you become more comfortable. Even just a few minutes of meditation can have significant benefits for quieting the mind and promoting relaxation.

Choose a Quiet Space: Find a quiet and comfortable space where you can practice meditation without distractions. Ideally, choose a space where you won't be interrupted and where you feel relaxed and at ease.

Set a Regular Schedule: Establish a regular meditation practice by setting aside a specific time each day for practice. Whether it's first thing in the morning, during your lunch break, or before bed, consistency is key to establishing a meditation routine.

Experiment with Different Techniques: Explore different types of meditation to find what works best for you. Whether you prefer mindfulness meditation, focused attention meditation, or loving-kindness meditation, there are many different techniques to choose from.

Use Guided Meditations: If you're new to meditation or find it difficult to quiet the mind on your own, consider using guided meditations. Guided meditations provide step-by-step instructions and can help you stay focused and engaged during your practice.

Be Patient and Persistent: Remember that meditation is a skill that takes time and practice to develop. Be patient with yourself and trust that with consistent practice, you will gradually experience greater peace, clarity, and stillness of mind.

Incorporating Meditation into Your Daily Routine:

Morning Meditation: Start your day with a short meditation practice to set a positive tone for the day ahead. Whether it's a few minutes of mindful breathing or a guided meditation on gratitude, taking time to quiet the mind in the morning can help you approach the day with greater clarity and calm.

Midday Meditation Break: Take a break during the middle of the day to recharge and refresh your mind with a short meditation practice. Whether it's a brief body scan meditation or a walking meditation around your office building, carving out time for meditation can help you maintain focus and productivity throughout the day.

Evening Wind-Down: Wind down in the evening with a relaxing meditation practice to quiet the mind and prepare for restful sleep. Whether it's a gentle yoga nidra meditation or a guided body relaxation meditation, taking time to unwind before bed can help you release tension and stress from the day and promote restful sleep.

Mindful Moments Throughout the Day: Incorporate mindfulness into your daily activities by bringing awareness to the present moment as you go about your day. Whether it's mindful eating, mindful walking, or mindful listening, finding moments of stillness and presence in your daily life can help you cultivate greater peace and clarity of mind.

Conclusion

In conclusion, meditation offers a powerful tool for quieting the mind, reducing stress, and promoting overall well-being. By incorporating meditation into your daily routine, you can cultivate a greater sense of inner peace, clarity, and resilience that positively impacts every aspect of your life. Whether you're new to meditation or an experienced practitioner, finding moments of stillness and presence in your daily life can help you navigate life's challenges with greater ease and grace. Experiment with different meditation techniques and strategies to find what works best for you, and remember that consistency and patience are key to experiencing the full benefits of meditation.

CHAPTER SIX

1. Embracing Imperfection - The Path to Self-Acceptance and Growth

Introduction

In a world that often values perfection and success above all else, embracing imperfection can feel like a radical act of rebellion. However, the reality is that perfection is an unattainable ideal, and the pursuit of it can lead to stress, anxiety, and dissatisfaction. Embracing imperfection is not about settling for mediocrity; rather, it's about acknowledging and accepting our inherent humanity, with all its flaws and vulnerabilities. In this chapter, we'll explore the importance of embracing imperfection, the benefits it brings to our lives, and practical strategies for cultivating self-acceptance and growth.

Understanding Imperfection

Imperfection is an inherent aspect of the human experience. No one is flawless, and striving for perfection is a futile endeavor that only leads to frustration and disappointment. Embracing imperfection means accepting ourselves and others as we are, with all our strengths and weaknesses, successes and failures, joys and sorrows.

Contrary to popular belief, imperfection is not a sign of weakness; rather, it's a source of strength and resilience. It's through our imperfections that we learn and grow, develop empathy and compassion, and forge authentic connections with others. Embracing imperfection is an essential step on the path to self-acceptance and fulfillment.

The Benefits of Embracing Imperfection:

Greater Self-Acceptance: Embracing imperfection allows us to accept ourselves as we are without judgment or criticism. When we let go of the need to be perfect, we free ourselves from the burden of self-doubt and insecurity, allowing us to embrace our true selves with love and compassion.

Reduced Stress and Anxiety: The pursuit of perfection is a major source of stress and anxiety for many people. When we embrace imperfection, we release ourselves from the constant pressure to measure up to impossible standards, leading to greater peace of mind and emotional well-being.

Improved Relationships: Embracing imperfection allows us to be more authentic and vulnerable in our relationships. When we let go of the facade of perfection, we create space for genuine connection and intimacy, fostering deeper and more meaningful relationships with others.

Fostering Creativity and Innovation: Imperfection is the birthplace of creativity and innovation. When we allow ourselves to make mistakes and take risks, we open ourselves up to new possibilities and discoveries, fueling our creativity and expanding our horizons.

Enhanced Resilience: Embracing imperfection builds resilience by teaching us to bounce back from setbacks and failures. When we accept that failure is a natural part of the learning process, we become more resilient in the face of adversity, able to persevere and grow stronger from our experiences.

Practical Strategies for Embracing Imperfection:

Practice Self-Compassion: Cultivate self-compassion by treating yourself with kindness, understanding, and acceptance, especially in moments of failure or struggle. Remind yourself that it's okay to be imperfect and that you are worthy of love and compassion just as you are.

Challenge Perfectionist Thinking: Notice and challenge perfectionist thoughts and beliefs that fuel feelings of inadequacy or self-doubt. Replace unrealistic expectations with more realistic and compassionate self-talk, focusing on progress rather than perfection.

Celebrate Mistakes and Failures: Shift your perspective on mistakes and failures from something to be feared or avoided to opportunities for growth and learning. Celebrate your mistakes as valuable lessons that contribute to your personal and professional development.

Practice Mindfulness: Cultivate present-moment awareness through mindfulness practices such as meditation, yoga, or deep breathing exercises. Mindfulness allows us to observe our thoughts and emotions without judgment, helping us develop greater acceptance and resilience in the face of imperfection.

Set Realistic Goals: Set realistic and achievable goals that allow for flexibility and adaptability. Instead of striving for perfection, focus on progress and improvement over time, celebrating small victories along the way.

Seek Support: Reach out to friends, family, or a therapist for support and encouragement on your journey to embracing imperfection. Surround yourself with people who accept you as you are and who encourage you to be your authentic self.

Embracing Imperfection in Practice:

Accepting Flaws and Vulnerabilities: Acknowledge and accept your flaws and vulnerabilities as natural and human. Instead of hiding or denying them, embrace them as integral parts of who you are, deserving of love and acceptance.

Letting Go of Comparison: Release yourself from the trap of comparison by focusing on your own journey and growth rather than comparing yourself to others. Remember that everyone has their own unique strengths and weaknesses, and there is no one-size-fits-all definition of success or perfection.

Finding Beauty in Imperfection: Embrace the beauty of imperfection by finding joy and inspiration in the imperfect and unconventional. Celebrate the quirks and idiosyncrasies that make you unique, and seek out beauty in unexpected places.

Taking Imperfect Action: Take imperfect action toward your goals and dreams, even if it means making mistakes or facing rejection. Remember that perfection is not a prerequisite for success and that taking imperfect action is better than not taking action at all.

Cultivating Gratitude: Cultivate gratitude for the imperfect moments and experiences that enrich your life and contribute to your growth and development. Practice gratitude for the lessons learned, the connections forged, and the opportunities for growth that arise from imperfection.

Conclusion

In conclusion, embracing imperfection is a powerful act of self-compassion and self-acceptance that can transform our lives in profound ways. By letting go of the need to be perfect and embracing our flaws and vulnerabilities, we open ourselves up to greater peace, joy, and fulfillment. Through practical strategies such as practicing self-compassion, challenging perfectionist thinking, and celebrating mistakes and failures, we can cultivate a greater sense of resilience, authenticity, and well-being. Embracing imperfection is not about settling for less; it's about embracing our humanity and recognizing that our imperfections are what make us beautifully and uniquely human.

2. Letting Go of Perfectionism and Unrealistic Expectations: Embracing Imperfection for a Fulfilling Life

Introduction

Perfectionism and unrealistic expectations are two common traps that many individuals fall into, often unknowingly, in their pursuit of success and happiness. While striving for excellence can be admirable, the relentless pursuit of perfection can lead to stress, anxiety, and dissatisfaction. In this chapter, we'll explore the detrimental effects of perfectionism and unrealistic expectations, why it's important to let go of them, and practical strategies for embracing imperfection and cultivating a more fulfilling life.

Understanding Perfectionism and Unrealistic Expectations

Perfectionism is a tendency to set excessively high standards for oneself and others, accompanied by a persistent fear of failure or criticism. Unrealistic expectations often go hand in hand with perfectionism, as individuals set impossibly high standards for themselves and others, leading to constant dissatisfaction and disappointment.

Perfectionism and unrealistic expectations can manifest in various areas of life, including work, relationships, and personal goals. Whether it's striving for flawless performance at work, seeking the perfect romantic partner, or expecting constant happiness and success, perfectionism and unrealistic expectations can take a toll on our mental and emotional well-being.

The Detrimental Effects of Perfectionism and Unrealistic Expectations:

Chronic Stress and Anxiety: Perfectionism and unrealistic expectations often lead to chronic stress and anxiety as individuals constantly strive to meet impossibly high standards. The fear of failure or falling short of expectations can create a constant sense of pressure and unease, leading to burnout and exhaustion.

Low Self-Esteem and Self-Criticism: Perfectionism fosters a sense of never feeling good enough, leading to low self-esteem and self-criticism. Individuals may harshly judge themselves for their perceived shortcomings and mistakes, leading to feelings of inadequacy and self-doubt.

Strained Relationships: Unrealistic expectations can strain relationships as individuals hold themselves and others to impossible standards. Constantly criticizing and nitpicking can create tension and resentment in relationships, leading to conflict and disconnection.

Procrastination and Avoidance: Perfectionism often leads to procrastination and avoidance as individuals fear taking action for fear of failure or criticism. Rather than risk falling short of expectations, individuals may delay tasks or avoid challenges altogether, further perpetuating feelings of inadequacy and frustration.

Limited Growth and Innovation: Perfectionism can stifle

creativity and innovation as individuals become overly focused on avoiding mistakes or imperfections. The fear of failure can prevent individuals from taking risks or trying new things, limiting their potential for growth and development.

Why It's Important to Let Go of Perfectionism and Unrealistic Expectations:

Greater Happiness and Fulfillment: Letting go of perfectionism and unrealistic expectations allows individuals to experience greater happiness and fulfillment in life. By embracing imperfection and accepting themselves and others as they are, individuals can find joy and satisfaction in the present moment rather than constantly striving for an unattainable ideal.

Reduced Stress and Anxiety: Releasing the pressure of perfectionism and unrealistic expectations reduces stress and anxiety, promoting greater mental and emotional well-being. By letting go of the need to be perfect, individuals can experience greater peace of mind and relaxation in their daily lives.

Stronger Relationships: Embracing imperfection fosters deeper and more meaningful connections with others. By accepting ourselves and others as imperfect beings, we create space for genuine empathy, compassion, and understanding in our relationships, fostering greater intimacy and connection.

Increased Resilience and Adaptability: Letting go of perfectionism and embracing imperfection builds resilience and adaptability in the face of challenges and setbacks. By accepting that failure is a natural part of the learning process, individuals become more resilient and better equipped to bounce back from adversity.

Enhanced Creativity and Innovation: Embracing imperfection unleashes creativity and innovation as individuals feel free to take risks and explore new ideas without fear of judgment or failure. By embracing experimentation and exploration, individuals can tap into their creative potential and bring new ideas to life.

Practical Strategies for Letting Go of Perfectionism and Unrealistic Expectations:

Set Realistic Goals: Set realistic and achievable goals that allow for flexibility and adaptability. Break larger goals down into smaller, manageable tasks, and celebrate progress rather than perfection.

Challenge Perfectionist Thinking: Notice and challenge perfectionist thoughts and beliefs that fuel feelings of inadequacy or self-doubt. Replace unrealistic expectations with more realistic and compassionate self-talk, focusing on progress rather than perfection.

Practice Self-Compassion: Cultivate self-compassion by treating yourself with kindness, understanding, and acceptance, especially in moments of failure or struggle. Remind yourself that it's okay to be imperfect and that you are worthy of love and compassion just as you are.

Embrace Mistakes and Failure: Shift your perspective on

mistakes and failures from something to be feared or avoided to opportunities for growth and learning. Celebrate your mistakes as valuable lessons that contribute to your personal and professional development.

Focus on the Process, Not the Outcome: Shift your focus from the end result to the process of learning and growth. Embrace the journey of self-discovery and personal development, trusting that progress is more important than perfection.

Practice Mindfulness: Cultivate present-moment awareness through mindfulness practices such as meditation, yoga, or deep breathing exercises. Mindfulness allows us to observe our thoughts and emotions without judgment, helping us develop greater acceptance and resilience in the face of imperfection.

Conclusion

In conclusion, letting go of perfectionism and unrealistic expectations is essential for cultivating a more fulfilling and meaningful life. By embracing imperfection and accepting ourselves and others as we are, we can experience greater happiness, resilience, and connection in our daily lives. Through practical strategies such as setting realistic goals, challenging perfectionist thinking, and practicing self-compassion, we can release the pressure of perfectionism and embrace the beauty of imperfection. By letting go of the need to be perfect, we can discover the joy and freedom that comes from living authentically and embracing life's imperfections.

3. Embracing Mistakes: Transforming Errors into Opportunities for Growth and Learning

Introduction

Mistakes are an inevitable part of the human experience, yet many of us fear them and go to great lengths to avoid them. However, mistakes are not failures; rather, they are valuable opportunities for growth and learning. By embracing mistakes and viewing them as stepping stones on the path to success, we can cultivate resilience, creativity, and a growth mindset. In this chapter, we'll explore the importance of embracing mistakes, the benefits they bring, and practical strategies for turning errors into opportunities for growth.

Understanding Mistakes

Mistakes are simply a natural part of the learning process. Whether it's a small error in judgment or a major setback, mistakes provide valuable feedback and insight that can help us improve and grow. Instead of viewing mistakes as something to be feared or avoided, we can choose to see them as opportunities for growth and development.

Mistakes can occur in various areas of life, including work, relationships, and personal goals. Whether it's a failed project at work, a misunderstanding with a loved one, or a missed opportunity, mistakes provide us with valuable lessons and experiences that contribute to our personal and professional development.

The Benefits of Embracing Mistakes:

Promotes Growth Mindset: Embracing mistakes promotes a growth mindset, which is the belief that abilities and intelligence can be developed through effort and practice. By viewing mistakes as opportunities for learning and improvement, individuals are more likely to persevere in the face of challenges and setbacks, leading to greater resilience and success.

Encourages Creativity and Innovation: Mistakes often lead to new insights and discoveries that can fuel creativity and innovation. When we're willing to take risks and experiment, we open ourselves up to new possibilities and ideas that can lead to breakthroughs and advancements in various fields.

Builds Resilience: Embracing mistakes builds resilience by teaching us to bounce back from setbacks and failures. By accepting that failure is a natural part of the learning process, individuals become more resilient and better equipped to handle adversity and challenges.

Fosters Self-Reflection and Self-Awareness: Mistakes provide opportunities for self-reflection and self-awareness, allowing individuals to gain insight into their strengths, weaknesses, and areas for improvement. By examining our mistakes and learning from them, we can develop greater self-awareness and make more informed decisions in the future.

Strengthens Relationships: Embracing mistakes fosters greater empathy and understanding in relationships. When we're willing to acknowledge our mistakes and take responsibility for them, we build trust and credibility with others, leading to stronger and more meaningful connections.

Practical Strategies for Embracing Mistakes:

Shift Your Perspective: Instead of viewing mistakes as failures, choose to see them as opportunities for growth and learning. Reframe mistakes as valuable experiences that contribute to your personal and professional development.

Practice Self-Compassion: Be kind and compassionate with yourself when you make mistakes. Treat yourself with the same kindness and understanding that you would offer to a friend, and remember that everyone makes mistakes from time to time.

Learn from Your Mistakes: Take the time to reflect on your mistakes and identify the lessons and insights they provide. What went wrong? What could you have done differently? Use your mistakes as opportunities to learn and grow, and apply those lessons to future endeavors.

Seek Feedback and Support: Don't be afraid to seek feedback and support from others when you make mistakes. Reach out to trusted friends, mentors, or colleagues for guidance and advice, and be open to constructive criticism that can help you improve.

Take Risks and Experiment: Don't let the fear of making mistakes hold you back from taking risks and trying new things. Embrace uncertainty and be willing to step outside of your comfort zone, knowing that mistakes are an inevitable part of the learning process.

Celebrate Progress, Not Perfection: Shift your focus from achieving perfection to making progress. Celebrate your efforts and accomplishments along the way, regardless of whether they're perfect or not. Remember that growth is a journey, not a destination.

Embracing Mistakes in Practice:

Learning from Failure: Instead of viewing failure as the end of the road, see it as a stepping stone on the path to success. Reflect on what went wrong, what you learned from the experience, and how you can apply those lessons to future endeavors.

Taking Calculated Risks: Don't be afraid to take calculated risks and try new things, even if there's a chance you might fail. Trust in your abilities and embrace the uncertainty that comes with stepping outside of your comfort zone.

Adapting to Change: Embrace mistakes as opportunities to adapt and evolve in response to changing circumstances. Instead of resisting change, be open to new possibilities and opportunities for growth that arise from unexpected challenges.

Building Resilience: Use mistakes as opportunities to build resilience and perseverance in the face of adversity. Instead of giving up when things don't go as planned, keep pushing forward and trust that you have the strength and resilience to overcome any obstacle.

Cultivating Creativity: Embrace mistakes as opportunities to unleash your creativity and innovation. Instead of seeing mistakes as setbacks, see them as opportunities to explore new ideas and approaches that can lead to breakthroughs and advancements.

Conclusion

In conclusion, embracing mistakes is essential for personal and professional growth. By viewing mistakes as opportunities for learning and improvement, we can cultivate resilience, creativity, and a growth mindset that empowers us to achieve our goals and fulfill our potential. Through practical strategies such as shifting our perspective, practicing self-compassion, and seeking feedback and support, we can embrace mistakes as valuable opportunities for growth and transform them into stepping stones on the path to success. Remember that mistakes are not failures; they're simply opportunities to learn, grow, and become the best version of ourselves.

4. Cultivating Self-Compassion and Acceptance: The Path to Inner Peace and Fulfillment

Introduction

Self-compassion and self-acceptance are foundational pillars of mental and emotional well-being. Yet, many of us struggle to treat ourselves with the same kindness, understanding, and acceptance that we offer to others. Instead, we may be plagued by self-criticism, judgment, and unrealistic expectations, leading to feelings of inadequacy and unworthiness. In this chapter, we'll explore the importance of cultivating self-compassion and acceptance, the benefits they bring, and practical strategies for embracing ourselves with love and compassion.

Understanding Self-Compassion and Acceptance

Self-compassion is the practice of treating ourselves with kindness, understanding, and care, especially in moments of struggle, failure, or suffering. It involves extending the same compassion to ourselves that we would offer to a friend in need, recognizing our common humanity and inherent worthiness.

Self-acceptance, on the other hand, is the practice of embracing ourselves as we are, with all our strengths and weaknesses, successes and failures, joys and sorrows. It involves letting go of the need to be perfect and recognizing that we are worthy of love and acceptance just as we are.

The Benefits of Self-Compassion and Acceptance:

Greater Emotional Resilience: Cultivating self-compassion and acceptance builds emotional resilience by providing a buffer against stress, anxiety, and depression. When we treat ourselves with kindness and understanding, we're better able to cope with life's challenges and setbacks, leading to greater emotional well-being.

Improved Mental Health: Self-compassion and acceptance are associated with improved mental health outcomes, including reduced symptoms of depression, anxiety, and low self-esteem. By embracing ourselves with love and acceptance, we create a nurturing inner environment that supports our mental and emotional well-being.

Enhanced Relationships: When we cultivate self-compassion and acceptance, we're better able to show up authentically in our relationships with others. By accepting ourselves as we are, we're more open and vulnerable with others, fostering deeper and more meaningful connections.

Increased Motivation and Resilience: Contrary to popular belief, self-compassion doesn't lead to complacency or laziness; rather, it fosters greater motivation and resilience. When we treat ourselves with kindness and understanding, we're more likely to pick ourselves up after failure and keep moving forward toward our goals.

Greater Life Satisfaction: Cultivating self-compassion and acceptance leads to greater life satisfaction and fulfillment. By embracing ourselves as we are and letting go of the need to be perfect, we're able to find joy and contentment in the present moment, regardless of external circumstances.

Practical Strategies for Cultivating Self-Compassion and Acceptance:

Practice Mindfulness: Cultivate present-moment awareness through mindfulness practices such as meditation, yoga, or deep breathing exercises. Mindfulness allows us to observe our thoughts and emotions without judgment, helping us develop greater self-awareness and self-compassion.

Challenge Negative Self-Talk: Notice and challenge negative self-talk and self-critical thoughts that undermine self-compassion and acceptance. Replace harsh self-judgments with more compassionate and realistic self-talk, focusing on kindness and understanding.

Practice Self-Kindness: Treat yourself with kindness and care, especially in moments of struggle or suffering. Offer yourself the same kindness and understanding that you would offer to a friend in need, recognizing your inherent worthiness and humanity.

Cultivate Gratitude: Cultivate gratitude for yourself and your unique qualities, strengths, and accomplishments. Take time each day to reflect on the things you appreciate about yourself, no matter how small or insignificant they may seem.

Set Realistic Expectations: Set realistic and achievable goals that allow for flexibility and self-compassion. Instead of striving for perfection, focus on progress and improvement over time, celebrating small victories along the way.

Practice Forgiveness: Practice forgiveness for yourself and others, letting go of past mistakes and grievances. Recognize that everyone makes mistakes and that holding onto resentment and self-blame only serves to perpetuate suffering.

Seek Support: Reach out to friends, family, or a therapist for support and encouragement on your journey to self-compassion and acceptance. Surround yourself with people who accept you as you are and who encourage you to embrace yourself with love and compassion.

Cultivating Self-Compassion and Acceptance in Practice:

Recognizing Your Humanity: Acknowledge your humanity and imperfections, recognizing that you are a flawed and imperfect being deserving of love and acceptance.

Embracing Imperfection: Embrace your imperfections as part of what makes you uniquely human, recognizing that you are worthy of love and acceptance just as you are.

Letting Go of Comparison: Release yourself from the trap of comparison by focusing on your own journey and growth rather than comparing yourself to others. Remember that everyone has their own unique strengths and weaknesses, and there is no one-size-fits-all definition of success or perfection.

Honoring Your Needs: Honor your needs and prioritize self-care, setting boundaries and saying no to things that deplete your energy or undermine your well-being. Remember that taking care of yourself is not selfish; it's essential for your mental and emotional health.

Celebrating Your Accomplishments: Celebrate your accomplishments and successes, no matter how small or insignificant they may seem. Acknowledge your efforts and achievements with gratitude and appreciation, recognizing the hard work and dedication that went into them.

Conclusion

In conclusion, cultivating self-compassion and acceptance is essential for mental and emotional well-being. By treating ourselves with kindness, understanding, and acceptance, we create a nurturing inner environment that supports our growth and development. Through practical strategies such as mindfulness, challenging negative self-talk, and practicing self-kindness, we can embrace ourselves with love and compassion and experience greater peace, joy, and fulfillment in our lives. Remember that you are worthy of love and acceptance just as you are and that embracing yourself with kindness and compassion is the key to unlocking your true potential and living a life of meaning and purpose.

CHAPTER SEVEN

7.1 Setting Boundaries and Priorities - Nurturing Self-Care and Respecting Your Needs

Introduction

In our fast-paced and interconnected world, setting boundaries and priorities is essential for maintaining balance, preserving mental and emotional well-being, and fostering healthy relationships. However, many of us struggle to assert our needs and prioritize our own self-care amidst the demands of work, relationships, and other responsibilities. In this chapter, we'll explore the importance of setting boundaries and priorities, the benefits they bring, and practical strategies for establishing healthy boundaries and aligning with our core values and goals.

Understanding Boundaries and Priorities

Boundaries are the limits we set for ourselves and others in order to protect our physical, emotional, and mental well-being. They define what is acceptable and unacceptable in our interactions with others, and they help us maintain a sense of autonomy and self-respect. Priorities, on the other hand, are the things that matter most to us and deserve our time, attention, and energy. They reflect our core values, goals, and aspirations, and they guide our decision-making and behavior.

The Benefits of Setting Boundaries and Priorities:

Preserves Mental and Emotional Well-Being: Setting boundaries and priorities helps us preserve our mental and emotional well-being by protecting us from overcommitment, burnout, and resentment. By asserting our needs and limits, we create space for self-care, rest, and relaxation, leading to greater peace and balance in our lives.

Fosters Healthy Relationships: Boundaries are essential for fostering healthy relationships with others. They help us communicate our needs and expectations clearly, establish mutual respect and understanding, and navigate conflicts and disagreements in a constructive manner.

Increases Productivity and Effectiveness: Prioritizing our tasks and commitments helps us increase our productivity and effectiveness by focusing on what matters most and eliminating distractions and time-wasters. By aligning our actions with our core values and goals, we can achieve greater success and fulfillment in our personal and professional lives.

Promotes Self-Respect and Empowerment: Setting boundaries and priorities promotes self-respect and empowerment by honoring our needs, values, and goals. When we assert our boundaries and prioritize our well-being, we send a message to ourselves and others that we are worthy of respect and consideration, empowering us to live authentically and pursue our passions and interests.

Practical Strategies for Setting Boundaries and Priorities:

Identify Your Core Values and Goals: Take time to reflect on your core values and goals in life. What matters most to you? What are your long-term aspirations and dreams? Clarifying your values and goals will help you prioritize your time, energy, and resources accordingly.

Communicate Your Needs Clearly: Practice assertive communication by expressing your needs, preferences, and boundaries clearly and respectfully. Use "I" statements to assert your boundaries and avoid blaming or criticizing others. Be firm and consistent in enforcing your boundaries, even if it means saying no to requests or invitations that don't align with your priorities.

Learn to Say No: Learn to say no to things that don't align with your values, goals, and priorities. Recognize that saying no is not selfish; it's an act of self-care and self-respect. Be honest and upfront with others about your limitations and boundaries, and don't feel guilty for prioritizing your well-being.

Set Limits and Boundaries: Set clear limits and boundaries around your time, energy, and resources. Determine how much time and energy you're willing to invest in various activities and commitments, and stick to those limits to avoid overcommitment and burnout. Delegate tasks when possible and say no to requests that exceed your capacity.

Practice Self-Care: Prioritize self-care and well-being by scheduling regular time for rest, relaxation, and activities that bring you joy and fulfillment. Make self-care a non-negotiable part of your routine, and don't sacrifice it for the sake of other commitments or obligations.

Evaluate and Adjust: Regularly evaluate your boundaries and priorities to ensure they align with your changing needs, values, and goals. Be willing to adjust your boundaries and priorities as necessary to maintain balance and alignment with what matters most to you.

Setting Boundaries and Priorities in Practice:

Protecting Your Time: Set boundaries around your time by prioritizing your most important tasks and commitments and saying no to distractions and time-wasters. Guard your time fiercely and allocate it mindfully to activities that align with your values and goals.

Nurturing Your Relationships: Set boundaries in your relationships by communicating your needs, expectations, and boundaries clearly and respectfully. Be assertive in expressing your limits and enforcing them, and be willing to walk away from relationships that violate your boundaries or compromise your well-being.

Honoring Your Well-Being: Prioritize your well-being by setting boundaries around self-care and rest. Make time for activities that nourish your mind, body, and soul, and don't hesitate to say no to things that deplete your energy or undermine your well-being.

Aligning with Your Values: Prioritize activities and

commitments that align with your core values and goals, and say no to things that don't contribute to your personal growth and fulfillment. Focus your time, energy, and resources on endeavors that bring you joy, meaning, and purpose.

Empowering Yourself: Recognize that setting boundaries and priorities is an act of self-empowerment and self-respect. Trust yourself to make decisions that honor your needs and values, and don't be afraid to assert yourself and advocate for what matters most to you.

Conclusion

In conclusion, setting boundaries and priorities is essential for preserving mental and emotional well-being, fostering healthy relationships, and aligning with our core values and goals. By clarifying our needs, communicating them assertively, and prioritizing our well-being, we create space for self-care, growth, and fulfillment in our lives. Through practical strategies such as identifying our core values and goals, learning to say no, and prioritizing self-care, we can establish healthy boundaries and priorities that honor our needs and empower us to live authentically and purposefully. Remember that setting boundaries and priorities is not selfish; it's an act of self-care and self-respect that allows us to show up fully in our lives and pursue our passions and interests with clarity and purpose.

7.2 The Importance of Setting Boundaries in Relationships and Work: Nurturing Healthy Dynamics and Personal Well-Being

Introduction

Boundaries serve as essential guidelines for maintaining healthy relationships and fostering productivity and well-being in the workplace. Yet, many individuals struggle to establish and maintain boundaries, leading to feelings of overwhelm, resentment, and burnout. In this chapter, we delve into the significance of setting boundaries in both personal and professional spheres, exploring their impact on mental and emotional health, interpersonal dynamics, and overall satisfaction.

Understanding Boundaries in Relationships and Work

Boundaries delineate the limits of acceptable behavior, delineating where one person's autonomy ends and another's begins. In relationships, boundaries define expectations, needs, and personal space, safeguarding against manipulation, co-dependency, and emotional strain. In the workplace, boundaries delineate professional roles, responsibilities, and work-life balance, mitigating stress, conflict, and dissatisfaction.

The Importance of Setting Boundaries in Relationships:

Preserve Autonomy and Individuality: Setting boundaries in relationships safeguards individual autonomy and personal identity, ensuring that each person's needs, values, and preferences are respected. By establishing clear boundaries, individuals can maintain a sense of self within the context of the relationship, fostering mutual respect and understanding.

Enhances Communication and Trust: Boundaries facilitate open and honest communication, allowing individuals to express their needs, concerns, and boundaries effectively. When boundaries are respected, trust and intimacy flourish, fostering a supportive and harmonious relationship dynamic.

Prevents Resentment and Conflict: Clear boundaries help prevent resentment and conflict by establishing clear expectations and limits. When boundaries are violated, individuals may feel disrespected or intruded upon, leading to tension and discord within the relationship. By setting and enforcing boundaries, individuals can address issues proactively and maintain healthy boundaries.

Promotes Emotional Well-Being: Boundaries are essential for preserving emotional well-being by protecting against emotional manipulation, coercion, and abuse. By asserting boundaries, individuals can safeguard their mental and emotional health, creating a safe and supportive environment for personal growth and fulfillment.

The Importance of Setting Boundaries in Work:

Maintains Work-Life Balance: Setting boundaries in the workplace is crucial for maintaining a healthy work-life balance. By delineating clear boundaries between work and personal life, individuals can prevent burnout, reduce stress, and preserve their overall well-being.

Fosters Productivity and Focus: Boundaries enhance productivity and focus by helping individuals prioritize tasks, manage time effectively, and minimize distractions. By setting boundaries around work hours, communication channels, and task priorities, individuals can optimize their performance and achieve their professional goals.

Promotes Respect and Professionalism: Boundaries promote respect and professionalism in the workplace by defining expectations, roles, and responsibilities clearly. When boundaries are respected, individuals feel valued and respected, fostering a positive and inclusive work culture.

Prevents Overwhelming and Burnout: Clear boundaries help prevent overwhelm and burnout by setting realistic limits on workload, availability, and responsibilities. By establishing boundaries around time, energy, and resources, individuals can avoid overcommitment and maintain sustainable levels of productivity and well-being.

Practical Strategies for Setting Boundaries in Relationships and Work:

Identify Your Needs and Limits: Take time to identify your needs, values, and limits in both relationships and work. Reflect on what is important to you, what you are willing to tolerate, and what you need to feel respected and supported.

Communicate Clearly and Assertively: Practice assertive communication by expressing your boundaries, needs, and expectations clearly and respectfully. Use "I" statements to convey your feelings and preferences, and be firm and consistent in enforcing your boundaries.

Set Boundaries Proactively: Set boundaries proactively before issues arise, rather than waiting until boundaries have been violated. Be proactive in communicating your boundaries and expectations to others, and address any concerns or conflicts that arise promptly and constructively.

Enforce Boundaries Consistently: Be consistent in enforcing your boundaries and expectations, even when it feels uncomfortable or challenging. Don't be afraid to assert yourself, advocate for your needs, and be prepared to set consequences if boundaries are violated.

Seek Support When Needed: Seek support from friends, family, or a therapist when setting and enforcing boundaries in relationships and work. Surround yourself with people who respect and support your boundaries, and don't hesitate to seek guidance and advice if you encounter challenges or resistance.

Setting Boundaries in Relationships and Work in Practice:

Communicating Personal Needs: Clearly communicate your personal needs, preferences, and boundaries to your partner, friends, and family members. Be honest and upfront about what you need to feel respected and supported in your relationships.

Establishing Work-Life Balance: Set boundaries around work hours, availability, and communication channels to maintain a healthy work-life balance. Create designated times for work, leisure, and self-care, and stick to them to prevent burnout and overwhelm.

Clarifying Roles and Responsibilities: Define roles and responsibilities clearly in the workplace to prevent confusion and conflict. Communicate expectations and boundaries with colleagues and supervisors, and be assertive in advocating for your needs and priorities.

Creating Physical and Emotional Space: Establish physical and emotional space in relationships and work to maintain autonomy and individuality. Set boundaries around personal space, privacy, and emotional intimacy, and respect others' boundaries in return.

Managing Technology and Communication: Set boundaries around technology and communication in both relationships and work. Establish guidelines for screen time, social media use, and email communication to prevent distractions and maintain focus.

Conclusion

In conclusion, setting boundaries is essential for maintaining healthy relationships, fostering productivity, and preserving mental and emotional well-being in both personal and professional contexts. By establishing clear boundaries and communicating them assertively, individuals can promote respect, trust, and understanding in their relationships and workplaces. Through practical strategies such as identifying needs and limits, communicating clearly, and seeking support when needed, individuals can cultivate boundaries that honor their needs and values, leading to greater satisfaction and fulfillment in all aspects of life. Remember that setting boundaries is not selfish; it's an act of self-care and self-respect that allows us to thrive personally and professionally while maintaining healthy connections with others.

7.3 Learning to Say No and Prioritize Effectively: Navigating Boundaries for Balance and Well-Being

Introduction

In today's fast-paced world filled with countless demands and obligations, learning to say no and prioritize effectively is essential for maintaining balance, preserving mental and emotional well-being, and achieving success in both personal and professional domains. However, many individuals struggle with assertiveness and boundary-setting, often saying yes to requests and commitments that overwhelm them and detract from their core priorities. In this chapter, we'll explore the importance of learning to say no and prioritize effectively, the benefits they bring, and practical strategies for navigating boundaries to enhance overall quality of life.

Understanding the Art of Saying No and Prioritization

Saying no is an act of setting boundaries and asserting one's needs, preferences, and limitations. It involves recognizing when a request or commitment doesn't align with one's values, goals, or capacity, and politely declining in a respectful and assertive manner.

Prioritization, on the other hand, is the process of determining what matters most and allocating time, energy, and resources accordingly. It involves identifying key objectives, goals, and responsibilities and organizing them in order of importance to ensure optimal focus and productivity.

The Importance of Saying No and Prioritizing Effectively:

Preserves Mental and Emotional Well-Being: Learning to say no and prioritize effectively is essential for preserving mental and emotional well-being. By setting boundaries and declining commitments that overwhelm or deplete us, we reduce stress, prevent burnout, and create space for self-care and relaxation.

Enhances Productivity and Focus: Prioritizing effectively allows us to focus our time and energy on tasks and activities that align with our goals and objectives. By saying no to distractions and non-essential tasks, we increase productivity, efficiency, and overall effectiveness in both personal and professional domains.

Fosters Healthy Relationships: Learning to say no is crucial for fostering healthy relationships with others. By asserting our boundaries and communicating our limitations clearly and respectfully, we establish mutual respect and understanding and cultivate relationships based on trust, authenticity, and reciprocity.

Promotes Self-Respect and Empowerment: Saying no and prioritizing effectively promotes self-respect and empowerment by honoring our needs, values, and goals. By recognizing our limitations and asserting our boundaries, we send a message to ourselves and others that we are worthy of respect and consideration and deserve to live according to our own priorities and aspirations.

Practical Strategies for Learning to Say No and Prioritize Effectively:

Clarify Your Values and Goals: Take time to clarify your core values, goals, and priorities in both personal and professional domains. Reflect on what matters most to you and what you want to achieve in different areas of your life, and use this clarity to guide your decision-making and boundary-setting.

Practice Assertive Communication: Develop assertiveness skills to communicate your needs, preferences, and limitations confidently and respectfully. Use "I" statements to express yourself clearly and assertively, and avoid apologizing or over-explaining your reasons for saying no.

Set Boundaries and Limits: Establish clear boundaries and limits around your time, energy, and resources to prevent overcommitment and burnout. Learn to recognize when your plate is full and politely decline additional requests or commitments that exceed your capacity.

Prioritize Tasks and Responsibilities: Use prioritization techniques such as the Eisenhower Matrix or ABC prioritization to identify key tasks and responsibilities and organize them based on urgency and importance. Focus your time and energy on high-priority tasks that align with your goals and objectives, and delegate or defer less critical tasks as needed.

Practice Self-Care: Prioritize self-care and well-being by scheduling regular time for rest, relaxation, and activities that recharge your batteries. Make self-care a non-negotiable part of your routine, and don't hesitate to say no to things that interfere with your self-care practices.

Learn to Delegate: Delegate tasks and responsibilities to others, when possible, to lighten your workload and free up time for higher-priority activities. Trust your colleagues, friends, or family members to handle tasks competently and effectively, and resist the urge to micromanage or control every aspect of a project or task.

Learning to Say No and Prioritize Effectively in Practice:

At Work: In the workplace, learning to say no and prioritize effectively is crucial for managing workload, meeting deadlines, and maintaining work-life balance. Practice assertive communication with colleagues and supervisors, and be transparent about your workload and availability. Prioritize tasks based on their impact and urgency, and delegate or defer non-essential tasks as needed to focus on high-priority responsibilities.

In Relationships: In personal relationships, setting boundaries and saying no is essential for maintaining healthy dynamics and preserving individual autonomy.

Communicate your needs and limitations openly and honestly with friends, family members, and romantic partners, and be willing to assert yourself when necessary to protect your well-being. Prioritize quality time with loved ones and activities that bring you joy and fulfillment, and don't hesitate to decline social invitations or commitments that don't align with your values or preferences.

With Yourself: Learning to say no and prioritize effectively also involves setting boundaries with yourself and managing internal expectations and pressures. Practice self-awareness and self-compassion, and be mindful of your own needs and limitations. Prioritize self-care and well-being, and don't hesitate to say no to self-imposed obligations or commitments that interfere with your mental and emotional health.

Conclusion

In conclusion, learning to say no and prioritize effectively is essential for maintaining balance, preserving mental and emotional well-being, and achieving success in both personal and professional domains. By setting boundaries, communicating our needs, and organizing our time and energy according to our priorities, we create space for self-care, focus, and fulfillment in our lives. Through practical strategies such as clarifying our values and goals, practicing assertive communication, and prioritizing tasks and responsibilities, we can navigate boundaries with confidence and empower ourselves to live authentically and purposefully. Remember that saying no is not selfish; it's an act of self-care and self-respect that allows us to honor our needs, values, and goals and create a life that aligns with our deepest aspirations and desires.

7.4 Strategies for Managing Time and Energy More Efficiently: Maximizing Productivity and Well-Being

Introduction

In our fast-paced and demanding world, managing time and energy effectively is crucial for achieving our goals, staying productive, and maintaining overall well-being. However, many of us struggle with time management and find ourselves overwhelmed by competing priorities and endless to-do lists. In this chapter, we'll explore practical strategies for managing time and energy more efficiently, optimizing productivity, and fostering greater balance and fulfillment in our lives.

Understanding Time and Energy Management

Time management involves the process of planning and organizing tasks and activities to make the most efficient use of available time. It includes setting goals, prioritizing tasks, and allocating time and resources effectively to accomplish objectives.

Energy management, on the other hand, focuses on optimizing our physical, mental, and emotional energy to enhance performance and well-being. It involves recognizing our energy levels and rhythms and aligning activities with our peak energy times to maximize productivity and focus.

The Importance of Efficient Time and Energy Management:

Enhances Productivity: Effective time and energy management increases productivity by enabling us to focus on high-priority tasks and eliminate time-wasting activities. By allocating our time and energy intentionally, we can accomplish more in less time and achieve our goals more efficiently.

Reduces Stress and Overwhelm: Proper time and energy management reduce stress and overwhelm by helping us stay organized and in control of our workload. By setting realistic goals and deadlines, we can avoid feeling overwhelmed by an endless list of tasks and responsibilities.

Improves Work-Life Balance: Efficient time and energy management improve work-life balance by allowing us to devote adequate time and energy to both professional and personal pursuits. By setting boundaries and prioritizing self-care, we can prevent burnout and maintain a healthy balance between work and leisure activities.

Fosters Well-Being: Managing time and energy effectively fosters overall well-being by promoting physical health, mental clarity, and emotional resilience. By prioritizing self-care activities such as exercise, relaxation, and social connection, we can recharge our batteries and maintain optimal levels of energy and vitality.

Strategies for Managing Time and Energy More Efficiently:

Set Clear Goals and Priorities: Clarify your short-term and long-term goals and prioritize tasks based on their importance and urgency. Break down larger goals into smaller, actionable steps, and focus on completing high-priority tasks that align with your objectives.

Create a Daily Schedule: Plan your day in advance by creating a daily schedule or to-do list outlining your tasks and commitments. Allocate specific blocks of time for each task, and be realistic about how long each task will take to complete. Schedule high-priority tasks during your peak energy times to maximize productivity and focus.

Use Time-Blocking Techniques: Time-blocking involves grouping similar tasks together and scheduling specific blocks of time to focus on them. Allocate uninterrupted periods of time for tasks that require deep focus and concentration, and minimize distractions such as email and social media during these blocks.

Practice the Pomodoro Technique: The Pomodoro Technique involves working in short bursts of focused activity (typically 25 minutes) followed by a short break. Set a timer for each work interval, and focus solely on the task at hand until the timer goes off. Take a short break to rest and recharge before starting the next work interval.

Delegate and Outsource Tasks: Identify tasks that can be delegated or outsourced to others to free up your time and energy for higher-priority activities. Delegate tasks to colleagues, family members, or virtual assistants who have the skills and resources to handle them effectively, and focus your efforts on tasks that require your unique expertise and attention.

Limit Multitasking: Avoid the temptation to multitask, as it can lead to decreased productivity and increased stress. Instead, focus on one task at a time and give it your full attention until it's completed.
By focusing on single-tasking, you'll be able to work more efficiently and produce higher-quality results.

Practice Self-Care: Prioritize self-care activities such as exercise, meditation, and relaxation to recharge your batteries and maintain optimal levels of energy and focus. Schedule regular breaks throughout the day to rest and recharge, and be mindful of your physical and mental well-being.

Set Boundaries: Establish clear boundaries around your time and energy to prevent burnout and overwhelm. Learn to say no to requests and commitments that don't align with your priorities, and set limits on how much time and energy you're willing to devote to certain tasks or activities.

Review and Reflect: Regularly review your time and energy management strategies to identify areas for improvement and reflection. Evaluate your progress toward your goals and adjust your approach as needed to stay on track and maintain balance and well-being.

Implementing Efficient Time and Energy Management in Practice:

At Work: In the workplace, efficient time and energy management are essential for maximizing productivity and performance. Set clear goals and priorities for your workday, and create a daily schedule outlining your tasks and commitments. Use time-blocking techniques to allocate focused time for important projects, and minimize distractions to maintain concentration and focus.

In Personal Life: In your personal life, efficient time and energy management help you maintain balance and fulfillment. Prioritize self-care activities such as exercise, relaxation, and social connection to recharge your batteries and prevent burnout. Set boundaries around your time and energy to prioritize activities that bring you joy and fulfillment, and delegate or outsource tasks when needed to free up your time for what matters most.

Balancing Work and Personal Life: Balancing work and personal life requires effective time and energy management to prevent burnout and maintain well-being. Set boundaries around your work hours and commitments, and prioritize self-care activities to maintain balance and fulfillment. Schedule regular breaks throughout the day to rest and recharge, and be mindful of your physical and mental well-being.

Conclusion

In conclusion, managing time and energy efficiently is essential for achieving goals, maximizing productivity, and maintaining overall well-being. By setting clear goals and priorities, creating a daily schedule, and using strategies such as time-blocking and the Pomodoro Technique, we can optimize our time and energy to accomplish more in less time. By practicing self-care, setting boundaries, and delegating tasks when needed, we can prevent burnout and maintain balance and fulfillment in both our personal and professional lives. Remember that effective time and energy management is not about doing more; it's about doing what matters most and living a life aligned with your values and priorities.

CHAPTER EIGHT

8.1 Cultivating Gratitude and Perspective - The Keys to Contentment and Resilience

Introduction

In a world often characterized by busyness, stress, and constant striving, cultivating gratitude and perspective is essential for fostering contentment, resilience, and overall well-being. Gratitude shifts our focus from what we lack to what we have, while perspective helps us see challenges as opportunities for growth and learning. In this chapter, we will explore the profound benefits of cultivating gratitude and perspective, as well as practical strategies for integrating these practices into our daily lives.

Understanding Gratitude and Perspective

Gratitude is the practice of acknowledging and appreciating the blessings and gifts in our lives, no matter how big or small. It involves cultivating a mindset of abundance and thankfulness, even in the face of adversity.

Perspective, on the other hand, is the ability to see situations from different angles and understand that challenges are temporary and can offer valuable lessons

134

and insights. It involves shifting our mindset from one of scarcity and limitation to one of possibility and growth.

The Importance of Cultivating Gratitude and Perspective:

Enhances Mental and Emotional Well-Being: Cultivating gratitude and perspective is linked to greater levels of happiness, life satisfaction, and overall well-being. By focusing on the positive aspects of our lives and reframing challenges as opportunities for growth, we can reduce stress, anxiety, and depression, and cultivate a greater sense of inner peace and contentment.

Promotes Resilience: Gratitude and perspective foster resilience by helping us cope with adversity and setbacks more effectively. By cultivating gratitude for the lessons and blessings that emerge from challenging experiences, we can bounce back more quickly and adapt more easily to change.

Strengthens Relationships: Expressing gratitude and adopting a positive perspective can strengthen relationships by fostering appreciation, connection, and empathy. When we acknowledge and express gratitude for the contributions of others, we deepen our relationships and create a supportive and uplifting social network.

Fosters Optimism and Hope: Gratitude and perspective cultivate optimism and hope by encouraging us to focus on the positive aspects of life and maintain a sense of possibility and optimism, even in difficult times. By adopting a growth mindset and viewing challenges as opportunities for growth, we can maintain a sense of hope and resilience in the face of adversity.

Practical Strategies for Cultivating Gratitude and Perspective:

Keep a Gratitude Journal: Take time each day to write down three things you are grateful for, no matter how small or seemingly insignificant. This practice helps train your brain to focus on the positive aspects of life and fosters a mindset of gratitude and abundance.

Practice Mindfulness: Cultivate present-moment awareness through mindfulness practices such as meditation, deep breathing, or mindful walking. Mindfulness helps us become more attuned to the present moment and appreciate the beauty and richness of life as it unfolds.

Reframe Challenges as Opportunities: When faced with adversity or setbacks, practice reframing challenges as opportunities for growth and learning. Ask yourself what lessons or insights you can glean from the experience, and focus on how you can grow stronger and wiser as a result.

Express Appreciation: Take time to express appreciation and gratitude to others for their kindness, support, and contributions. Send a handwritten thank you note, make a phone call, or simply express your gratitude in person. Showing appreciation not only strengthens your relationships but also boosts your own sense of well-being.

Practice Self-Compassion: Be kind and compassionate

toward yourself, especially during difficult times. Treat yourself with the same kindness and understanding that you would offer to a friend in need, and remind yourself that challenges are a natural part of life and an opportunity for growth and learning.

Seek Perspective: When faced with challenges or difficulties, seek perspective by considering the bigger picture. Ask yourself how the situation will matter in the grand scheme of your life, or reflect on how others have overcome similar challenges. Shifting your perspective can help you see challenges as temporary and manageable.

Count Your Blessings: Take time each day to reflect on the blessings and gifts in your life, such as your health, relationships, and opportunities. Cultivate an attitude of gratitude by counting your blessings and appreciating the abundance that surrounds you.

Practice Acts of Kindness: Engage in acts of kindness and generosity toward others, whether through volunteering, helping a friend in need, or simply offering a kind word or gesture. Acts of kindness not only benefit others but also cultivate a sense of gratitude and connection within yourself.

Cultivating Gratitude and Perspective in Practice:

In Daily Life: Incorporate gratitude and perspective into your daily routine by starting and ending each day with a moment of reflection. Take a few minutes in the morning to express gratitude for the day ahead, and before bed, reflect on the blessings and lessons of the day. Practice mindfulness throughout the day by bringing your attention to the present moment and appreciating the beauty and richness of life as it unfolds.

In Relationships: Strengthen your relationships by expressing gratitude and appreciation to those you care about. Take time to acknowledge their contributions and support, and express your gratitude for the positive impact they have on your life. Practice active listening and empathy to deepen your connections and cultivate a sense of mutual appreciation and understanding.

In Adversity: When faced with challenges or setbacks, practice gratitude and perspective by reframing the situation as an opportunity for growth and learning. Seek support from others and draw on your inner resilience and strength to navigate the challenges with grace and resilience. Remember that challenges are temporary and can offer valuable lessons and insights that contribute to your personal growth and development.

Conclusion

In conclusion, cultivating gratitude and perspective is essential for fostering contentment, resilience, and overall well-being. By focusing on the positive aspects of life and reframing challenges as opportunities for growth, we can reduce stress, increase happiness, and cultivate a greater sense of inner peace and fulfillment. Through practical strategies such as keeping a gratitude journal, practicing mindfulness, and expressing appreciation to others, we can integrate gratitude and perspective into our daily lives and experience the profound benefits they bring. Remember that gratitude is not only a state of mind but also a way of life, and by cultivating gratitude and perspective, we can live more fully and authentically, no matter what life may bring.

8.2 Shifting Focus from Problems to Blessings: Cultivating Gratitude and Perspective

Introduction

In the hustle and bustle of daily life, it's easy to get caught up in our problems and challenges, allowing them to consume our thoughts and emotions. However, by shifting our focus from problems to blessings, we can cultivate gratitude and gain a new perspective on life. In this chapter, we'll explore the transformative power of gratitude, the benefits of shifting focus, and practical strategies for fostering a mindset of appreciation and abundance.

Understanding the Power of Gratitude:

Gratitude is the practice of recognizing and appreciating the good things in our lives, both big and small. It involves acknowledging the blessings, opportunities, and privileges we have and expressing appreciation for them.

Gratitude has been linked to numerous physical, mental, and emotional benefits, including improved mood, reduced stress, enhanced resilience, and greater overall well-being. By cultivating gratitude, we shift our focus from scarcity and lack to abundance and fulfillment, and we invite more positive experiences into our lives.

The Benefits of Shifting Focus from Problems to Blessings:

Improves Mental and Emotional Well-Being: Shifting our focus from problems to blessings improves our mental and emotional well-being by reducing stress, anxiety, and depression. By acknowledging the good things in our lives, we cultivate a sense of optimism, hope, and joy that uplifts our spirits and enhances our overall mood.

Enhances Resilience and Coping Skills: Practicing gratitude enhances resilience and coping skills by helping us navigate challenges and setbacks with grace and perspective. By focusing on the blessings and lessons in difficult situations, we find strength and wisdom that empower us to overcome obstacles and grow from adversity.

Strengthens Relationships: Gratitude strengthens relationships by fostering appreciation, kindness, and connection with others. By expressing gratitude for the people in our lives and the positive experiences we share, we deepen our bonds and create a supportive network of love and appreciation.

Promotes Physical Health: Gratitude has been linked to numerous physical health benefits, including improved sleep, reduced inflammation, and enhanced immune function. By cultivating gratitude, we reduce the impact of stress on our bodies and promote overall health and vitality.

Increases Happiness and Life Satisfaction: Shifting our

focus from problems to blessings increases happiness and life satisfaction by fostering a sense of fulfillment and contentment. By recognizing the abundance and beauty in our lives, we experience greater joy and gratitude for the present moment.

Practical Strategies for Shifting Focus from Problems to Blessings:

Keep a Gratitude Journal: Start a daily or weekly gratitude journal where you write down things you're grateful for. Reflect on the blessings, big and small, that you've experienced each day, and express appreciation for them in writing. Cultivate a habit of gratitude by making it a regular part of your routine.

Practice Mindfulness: Cultivate present-moment awareness through mindfulness practices such as meditation, yoga, or deep breathing exercises. Notice the beauty and abundance around you, and savor the simple pleasures of life. By being fully present, you can shift your focus from worries and concerns to the richness of the present moment.

Count Your Blessings: Take time each day to consciously count your blessings and appreciate the good things in your life. Reflect on the people, experiences, and opportunities that bring you joy and fulfillment, and express gratitude for them verbally or in writing. By acknowledging your blessings, you invite more abundance and positivity into your life.

Focus on What You Can Control: Instead of dwelling on

problems and challenges that are beyond your control, focus on what you can control and influence in your life. Shift your energy toward proactive solutions and positive actions that empower you to make a difference and create positive change.

Practice Random Acts of Kindness: Spread gratitude and positivity by practicing random acts of kindness toward others. Express appreciation for the people in your life through kind words, gestures, or acts of service. By brightening someone else's day, you also uplift your own spirits and cultivate a sense of abundance and generosity.

Shift Your Perspective: Challenge negative thinking patterns and cultivate a mindset of abundance and possibility. Instead of viewing setbacks as failures, see them as opportunities for growth and learning. Look for the silver lining in difficult situations and focus on the lessons and blessings they bring.

Connect with Nature: Spend time in nature and immerse yourself in the beauty and wonder of the natural world. Take walks in the park, hike in the mountains, or simply sit and observe the beauty of the sunrise or sunset. Nature has a way of grounding us and reminding us of the abundance and beauty that surrounds us.

Practice Gratitude Rituals: Create rituals or routines that reinforce gratitude and appreciation in your life. Start or end each day with a gratitude prayer or meditation, or gather with loved ones for a gratitude circle where you share blessings and positive experiences. By incorporating gratitude into your daily life, you create a culture of appreciation and abundance that enriches your relationships and overall well-being.

Shifting Focus from Problems to Blessings in Practice:

In Daily Life: In your daily life, practice gratitude by consciously shifting your focus from problems to blessings. Start each day with a gratitude practice, such as writing in a gratitude journal or reciting a gratitude prayer. Throughout the day, pause to notice the blessings and beauty around you, and express appreciation for them in the moment.

In Relationships: In your relationships, cultivate gratitude by expressing appreciation for the people in your life and the positive experiences you share. Take time to acknowledge the efforts and contributions of others and express gratitude for their support and friendship. By nurturing a culture of gratitude in your relationships, you strengthen your bonds and create a sense of connection and belonging.

In Challenges and Setbacks: In times of challenges and setbacks, practice gratitude by focusing on the lessons and blessings they bring. Look for opportunities for growth and learning, and express appreciation for the strength and resilience they cultivate within you. By reframing difficulties as opportunities for growth, you can navigate challenges with grace and perspective.

In Celebrations and Victories: In moments of celebration and victory, practice gratitude by acknowledging the blessings and abundance in your life. Take time to savor your successes and express gratitude for the people who supported you along the way. By celebrating your achievements with gratitude, you invite more abundance and success into your life.

Conclusion

In conclusion, shifting our focus from problems to blessings is a powerful practice that cultivates gratitude, enhances well-being, and fosters a deeper sense of fulfillment and joy. By acknowledging the blessings in our lives and expressing appreciation for them, we shift our perspective from scarcity and lack to abundance and gratitude. Through practical strategies such as keeping a gratitude journal, practicing mindfulness, and focusing on what we can control, we can cultivate a mindset of appreciation and abundance that enriches every aspect of our lives. Remember that gratitude is not just a fleeting feeling; it's a way of being that transforms our relationship with ourselves, others, and the world around us.

8.3 Practicing Gratitude Exercises to Rewire the Brain: Cultivating Positivity and Well-Being

Introduction

Gratitude is a powerful practice that can transform our lives by shifting our focus from what we lack to what we have. By cultivating an attitude of gratitude, we can rewire our brains to perceive the world through a lens of abundance and positivity. In this chapter, we'll explore various gratitude exercises designed to rewire the brain, enhance well-being, and promote a deeper sense of appreciation for life's blessings.

Understanding the Neuroscience of Gratitude

Neuroscience research has shown that practicing gratitude can have profound effects on the brain's structure and function. Gratitude activates regions of the brain associated with reward processing, empathy, and social bonding, leading to increased feelings of happiness, connection, and well-being.

Gratitude also stimulates the production of neurotransmitters such as dopamine and serotonin, which are associated with pleasure and mood regulation. By regularly practicing gratitude, we can strengthen neural pathways associated with positive emotions and resilience, making it easier to maintain a positive outlook even in the face of challenges.

The Benefits of Practicing Gratitude Exercises:

Enhances Mental and Emotional Well-Being: Practicing gratitude exercises enhances mental and emotional well-being by promoting feelings of happiness, contentment, and peace. By focusing on the positive aspects of our lives, we can reduce stress, anxiety, and depression and cultivate a greater sense of resilience and optimism.

Strengthens Relationships: Gratitude exercises strengthen relationships by fostering appreciation, empathy, and connection with others. By expressing gratitude for the people in our lives and the positive experiences we share, we deepen our bonds and create a supportive network of love and appreciation.

Improves Physical Health: Gratitude has been linked to numerous physical health benefits, including improved sleep, reduced inflammation, and enhanced immune function. By cultivating gratitude, we reduce the impact of stress on our bodies and promote overall health and vitality.

Increases Resilience: Practicing gratitude exercises increases resilience by helping us navigate challenges and setbacks with grace and perspective. By focusing on the blessings and lessons in difficult situations, we can find strength and wisdom that empower us to overcome obstacles and grow from adversity.

Promotes Generosity and Kindness: Gratitude exercises promote generosity and kindness by inspiring us to pay it forward and spread positivity to others. By expressing gratitude for the kindnesses we receive, we are more likely to extend kindness to others, creating a ripple effect of goodness in the world.

Practical Gratitude Exercises to Rewire the Brain:

Gratitude Journaling: Keep a daily gratitude journal where you write down three things you're grateful for each day. Reflect on the blessings, big and small, that you've experienced, and express appreciation for them in writing. Cultivate a habit of gratitude by making journaling a regular part of your routine.

Gratitude Letter: Write a letter expressing gratitude to someone who has had a positive impact on your life. Be specific about what you appreciate about them and how their actions have made a difference for you. If possible, deliver the letter in person and read it aloud to the recipient to deepen the connection and appreciation.

Gratitude Walk: Take a gratitude walk in nature and immerse yourself in the beauty and wonder of the natural world. Notice the sights, sounds, and sensations around you, and express gratitude for the abundance of life and beauty that surrounds you. Allow yourself to be fully present and open to the blessings of the present moment.

Three Good Things: At the end of each day, reflect on three good things that happened and why they happened. Focus on the positive aspects of your day, no matter how small, and express gratitude for them. This exercise helps rewire the brain to notice and appreciate the good things in life, even during challenging times.

Gratitude Meditation: Practice gratitude meditation by focusing your attention on feelings of gratitude and appreciation. Sit quietly and bring to mind the people, experiences, and blessings you're grateful for. Notice how these thoughts make you feel and cultivate a sense of warmth and gratitude in your heart.

Gratitude Jar: Create a gratitude jar where you write down things you're grateful for on slips of paper throughout the year. Whenever you need a boost of positivity, reach into the jar and read a few notes of gratitude. This exercise serves as a visual reminder of the abundance and blessings in your life.

Gratitude Rituals: Create rituals or routines that reinforce gratitude and appreciation in your life. Start or end each day with a gratitude prayer or meditation, or gather with loved ones for a gratitude circle where you share blessings and positive experiences. By incorporating gratitude into your daily life, you create a culture of appreciation and abundance that enriches your relationships and overall well-being.

Conclusion

In conclusion, practicing gratitude exercises is a powerful way to rewire the brain, enhance well-being, and cultivate a deeper sense of appreciation for life's blessings. By regularly focusing on the positive aspects of our lives and expressing appreciation for them, we strengthen neural pathways associated with gratitude and happiness and foster a more positive outlook on life. Through practical exercises such as gratitude journaling, gratitude letters, and gratitude walks, we can cultivate a mindset of abundance and positivity that enriches every aspect of our lives. Remember that gratitude is not just a fleeting feeling; it's a way of being that transforms our relationship with ourselves, others, and people around the world.

8.4 Gaining Perspective Through Mindfulness and Self-Reflection: Cultivating Clarity and Wisdom

Introduction

In the fast-paced modern world, it's easy to get caught up in the chaos of daily life, losing sight of what truly matters and feeling overwhelmed by stress and uncertainty. However, by cultivating mindfulness and engaging in self-reflection, we can gain a deeper perspective on our experiences, thoughts, and emotions, allowing us to navigate life's challenges with greater clarity, wisdom, and resilience. In this chapter, we'll explore the transformative power of mindfulness and self-reflection, the benefits they bring, and practical strategies for incorporating these practices into our lives to gain perspective and foster personal growth.

Understanding Mindfulness and Self-Reflection

Mindfulness is the practice of paying attention to the present moment with openness, curiosity, and acceptance. It involves tuning into our thoughts, feelings, and sensations without judgment and cultivating a sense of awareness and presence in our everyday experiences.

Self-reflection, on the other hand, is the process of examining our thoughts, feelings, and behaviors in a deeper and more intentional way. It involves stepping back from our experiences and observing them with curiosity and compassion, gaining insight into our patterns, motivations, and values.

The Benefits of Mindfulness and Self-Reflection:

Enhances Clarity and Insight: Practicing mindfulness and self-reflection enhances clarity and insight by allowing us to see our experiences and ourselves more clearly. By observing our thoughts and emotions without attachment, we gain perspective on our patterns and habits and develop a deeper understanding of ourselves and the world around us.

Reduces Stress and Anxiety: Mindfulness and self-reflection have been shown to reduce stress and anxiety by promoting relaxation, inner calm, and emotional regulation. By cultivating awareness of our thoughts and emotions, we can break free from automatic patterns of reactivity and respond to challenges with greater equanimity and resilience.

Promotes Emotional Well-Being: Engaging in mindfulness and self-reflection promotes emotional well-being by fostering self-awareness, self-compassion, and acceptance. By acknowledging and honoring our emotions without judgment, we create space for healing and growth and cultivate a greater sense of peace and contentment in our lives.

Improves Relationships: Mindfulness and self-reflection improve relationships by fostering empathy, compassion, and authentic communication. By becoming more attuned to our own thoughts and emotions, we develop a deeper understanding and appreciation of others and cultivate more meaningful and authentic connections.

Fosters Personal Growth: Mindfulness and self-reflection foster personal growth by encouraging self-discovery, learning, and evolution. By exploring our inner landscape with curiosity and openness, we uncover hidden talents, strengths, and aspirations and align more fully with our values and purpose in life.

Practical Strategies for Gaining Perspective Through Mindfulness and Self-Reflection:

Mindful Breathing: Practice mindful breathing by focusing your attention on the sensation of your breath as it flows in and out of your body. Notice the rise and fall of your chest or the sensation of air passing through your nostrils. Whenever your mind wanders, gently guide your attention back to your breath, anchoring yourself in the present moment.

Body Scan Meditation: Engage in a body scan meditation by systematically bringing awareness to each part of your body, starting from your toes and moving upwards toward your head. Notice any sensations, tensions, or areas of discomfort without judgment, and allow them to soften and release with each breath.

Mindful Walking: Practice mindful walking by taking slow, deliberate steps and paying attention to the sensations of movement in your body. Notice the feeling of your feet connecting with the ground, the rhythm of your breath, and the sights and sounds around you. Allow yourself to be fully present in each moment as you move through space.

Journaling: Engage in reflective journaling by writing about your thoughts, feelings, and experiences in a journal or notebook. Take time each day to reflect on your day, noting any insights, challenges, or moments of gratitude. Use journaling as a tool for self-exploration and self-expression, allowing your innermost thoughts and feelings to flow freely onto the page.

Mindful Eating: Practice mindful eating by savoring each bite of food and paying attention to the flavors, textures, and sensations in your mouth. Notice any thoughts or emotions that arise as you eat, and observe your hunger and fullness cues without judgment. Cultivate a sense of gratitude for the nourishment and sustenance that food provides.

Reflection Questions: Ask yourself reflective questions to deepen your self-awareness and gain perspective on your experiences. For example, you might ask yourself, "What am I grateful for today?" "What lessons can I learn from this situation?" or "What values are most important to me at this moment?"

Silent Retreats: Consider attending a silent retreat or retreat center where you can immerse yourself in mindfulness practices and self-reflection away from the distractions of everyday life. Use this time for deep introspection and contemplation, allowing yourself to connect with your inner wisdom and intuition.

Mindful Listening: Practice mindful listening by giving your full attention to the speaker without interrupting or judging. Focus on truly understanding their perspective and empathizing with their experience. Notice any impulses to react or respond, and allow yourself to listen with an open heart and mind.

Gaining Perspective Through Mindfulness and Self-Reflection in Practice:

In Daily Life: In your daily life, practice mindfulness and self-reflection by integrating these practices into your routines and activities. Take moments throughout the day to pause and check in with yourself, noticing your thoughts, feelings, and sensations without judgment. Use reflective questions or journaling prompts to deepen your self-awareness and gain perspective on your experiences.

In Relationships: In your relationships, practice mindful communication and active listening to deepen your connections with others. Take time to truly listen to their perspectives and experiences, and respond with empathy and understanding. Use mindfulness and self-reflection to cultivate greater compassion and appreciation for the people in your life.

In Challenges and Setbacks: In times of challenges and setbacks, use mindfulness and self-reflection as tools for resilience and growth. Take time to explore your thoughts and emotions surrounding the situation, and look for opportunities for learning and growth. Cultivate a sense of curiosity and openness to new perspectives, and trust in your ability to navigate difficulties with grace and wisdom.

In Moments of Joy and Gratitude: In moments of joy and gratitude, use mindfulness and self-reflection to savor the experience fully and appreciate the blessings in your life. Take time to notice the feelings of happiness and fulfillment that arise, and express gratitude for the people, experiences, and opportunities that bring you joy. Use these moments as reminders of the abundance and beauty that surround you, even in the midst of life's challenges.

Conclusion

In conclusion, gaining perspective through mindfulness and self-reflection is a powerful practice that cultivates clarity, wisdom, and resilience in the face of life's challenges. By tuning into the present moment with openness and curiosity and exploring our inner landscape with compassion and self-awareness, we gain insight into our thoughts, emotions, and behaviors and deepen our understanding of ourselves and the world around us through practical strategies such as mindful breathing, body scan meditations, mindful walking, mindful listening.

CHAPTER NINE

9.1 Seeking Support and Connection: Navigating Life's Challenges Together

Introduction

In times of difficulty and uncertainty, seeking support and connection is essential for navigating life's challenges with resilience and grace. Whether facing personal struggles, professional setbacks, or emotional upheaval, having a supportive network of friends, family, and community can provide comfort, guidance, and strength. In this chapter, we'll explore the importance of seeking support and connection, the benefits they bring, and practical strategies for fostering meaningful relationships and building a supportive network.

Understanding the Importance of Seeking Support and Connection

Seeking support and connection is vital for our mental, emotional, and physical well-being. Humans are inherently social beings, wired for connection and belonging. When we face challenges or adversity, having a supportive network of people who care about us can provide emotional validation, practical assistance, and a sense of belonging that buffers against stress and promotes resilience.

The Benefits of Seeking Support and Connection:

Emotional Support: Seeking support and connection provides emotional validation, empathy, and understanding during times of distress. Having someone to listen, empathize, and offer words of encouragement can alleviate feelings of loneliness and isolation and provide comfort and reassurance in times of need.

Practical Assistance: Supportive relationships offer practical assistance and resources to help us cope with life's challenges more effectively. Whether it's lending a listening ear, offering advice, or providing tangible help such as childcare, transportation, or financial assistance, having a support network can lighten the burden and make it easier to navigate difficult circumstances.

Validation and Affirmation: Connecting with others validates our experiences and feelings, affirming our worth and value as individuals. Sharing our struggles and vulnerabilities with others helps us feel seen, heard, and understood, reducing feelings of shame or inadequacy and promoting self-acceptance and self-compassion.

Perspective and Insight: Seeking support and connection allows us to gain perspective and insight from others who may have faced similar challenges or experiences. Hearing different viewpoints and perspectives can broaden our understanding of a situation, offer new solutions or coping strategies, and inspire hope and resilience.

Stress Reduction: Supportive relationships act as a buffer against stress, helping to reduce the physiological and psychological impact of challenging circumstances. Connecting with others activates the body's relaxation response, lowering levels of stress hormones and promoting feelings of calm and well-being.

Practical Strategies for Seeking Support and Connection:

Reach Out to Trusted Individuals: Identify trusted individuals in your life whom you feel comfortable confiding in and seeking support from. This may include close friends, family members, mentors, or colleagues whom you trust and respect. Reach out to them when you need a listening ear, emotional support, or practical assistance.

Join Support Groups: Consider joining support groups or community organizations that cater to individuals facing similar challenges or experiences. Whether it's a support group for individuals coping with grief, addiction, chronic illness, or life transitions, connecting with others who share your struggles can provide validation, understanding, and a sense of belonging.

Seek Professional Help: Don't hesitate to seek professional help from therapists, counselors, or support services when needed. Mental health professionals can offer expert guidance, support, and resources to help you navigate difficult emotions, develop coping skills, and work through challenging life circumstances.

Engage in Community Activities: Get involved in community activities, volunteer work, or social gatherings that align with your interests and values. Connecting with like-minded individuals and contributing to causes larger than yourself fosters a sense of belonging and purpose while providing opportunities for meaningful connection and support.

Utilize Online Resources: Explore online resources, forums, and virtual support groups that cater to specific needs or interests. Online communities offer a platform for connecting with others from diverse backgrounds and geographic locations, providing a sense of camaraderie and support, particularly for individuals who may feel isolated or marginalized in their offline communities.

Practice Active Listening: Be a supportive presence for others by practicing active listening and empathy. Listen attentively to their concerns, validate their feelings, and offer non-judgmental support and encouragement. Sometimes, all it takes is a compassionate listener to make a significant difference in someone's life.

Offer Support to Others: Extend a helping hand to others in need by offering your support, empathy, and assistance. Whether it's checking in on a friend going through a tough time, offering to lend a helping hand, or simply being present and available, acts of kindness and compassion strengthen bonds and foster reciprocal support within communities.

Create Healthy Boundaries: While seeking support and connection is essential, it's also important to create healthy boundaries to protect your well-being. Be mindful of your own needs and limitations, and communicate them assertively with others. Prioritize self-care and seek support from individuals who respect and honor your boundaries.

Seeking Support and Connection in Practice:

In Times of Crisis: In times of crisis or emotional distress, don't hesitate to reach out to your support network for help and guidance. Whether it's a trusted friend, family member, or mental health professional, seeking support can provide the emotional validation and practical assistance you need to cope with difficult emotions and circumstances.

During Major Life Transitions: Major life transitions, such as job changes, relocations, or relationship upheavals, can be challenging to navigate alone. Seek support and connection from trusted individuals who can offer guidance, encouragement, and perspective during times of change and uncertainty.

For Mental Health Concerns: If you're struggling with mental health concerns such as anxiety, depression, or trauma, don't hesitate to reach out to mental health professionals for help. Therapists, counselors, and support groups can offer specialized support and resources to help you cope with difficult emotions and develop healthy coping strategies.

For Personal Growth: Seeking support and connection isn't just for times of crisis; it's also essential for personal growth and self-discovery. Surround yourself with individuals who inspire and uplift you, and engage in meaningful conversations and activities that nurture your personal and spiritual development.

Conclusion

In conclusion, seeking support and connection is essential for navigating life's challenges with resilience, compassion, and grace. By reaching out to trusted individuals, joining support groups, and engaging in community activities, we cultivate meaningful relationships and build a supportive network that provides emotional validation, practical assistance, and perspective during difficult times. Remember that seeking support isn't a sign of weakness; it's a courageous act of self-care and self-compassion that strengthens bonds and fosters growth and resilience. As we journey through life's ups and downs, let us lean on each other for support and, in doing so, create a world where connection and compassion flourish.

9.2 The Value of Seeking Support from Friends, Family, or Professionals: Nurturing Resilience and Well-Being

Introduction

In times of uncertainty, stress, or adversity, seeking support from friends, family, or professionals can be a lifeline that helps us navigate challenges with greater resilience and well-being. Whether facing personal struggles, professional setbacks, or mental health concerns, reaching out for support allows us to share our burdens, gain new perspectives, and access resources that empower us to cope and thrive. In this chapter, we'll delve into the profound value of seeking support from various sources, exploring how it nurtures resilience, fosters growth, and promotes overall well-being.

The Importance of Seeking Support:

Validation and Understanding: Seeking support provides validation and understanding of our experiences, feelings, and struggles. When we share our challenges with others, they can offer empathy, compassion, and reassurance, helping us feel seen, heard, and understood.

Emotional Outlet: Talking about our feelings and experiences with supportive individuals serves as an emotional outlet, allowing us to express ourselves authentically and release pent-up emotions. This process can be cathartic and healing, reducing feelings of stress, anxiety, and isolation.

Perspective and Insight: Seeking support offers an opportunity to gain new perspectives and insights on our challenges. Friends, family, or professionals may offer fresh viewpoints, alternative solutions, or practical advice that we hadn't considered, broadening our understanding and empowering us to make informed decisions.

Practical Assistance: Supportive individuals can offer practical assistance and resources to help us navigate challenging circumstances. Whether it's lending a listening ear, providing tangible help such as childcare or transportation, or connecting us with relevant services or professionals, their support can ease our burden and facilitate problem-solving.

Building Resilience: Seeking support nurtures resilience by reinforcing our sense of connectedness and belonging. Knowing that we have a supportive network of people who care about us fosters a sense of security and confidence, enabling us to weather life's storms with greater strength and resilience.

Promoting Self-Care: Seeking support encourages self-care by reminding us of the importance of prioritizing our well-being. When we reach out for support, we acknowledge our own needs and take proactive steps to address them, whether it's through seeking therapy, setting boundaries, or engaging in self-care practices.

The Value of Support from Friends and Family:

Unconditional Love and Acceptance: Friends and family offer unconditional love and acceptance, creating a safe space where we can be ourselves without fear of judgment or rejection. Their unwavering support reminds us that we are valued and cherished, bolstering our self-esteem and sense of belonging.

Shared History and Connection: Friends and family share a unique bond forged by shared experiences, memories, and connections. They understand our background, values, and aspirations, providing a sense of continuity and connection that nurtures our sense of identity and belonging.

Accessibility and Availability: Friends and family are often readily accessible and available when we need support, whether it's through a phone call, text message, or in-person visit. Their proximity and familiarity make them reliable sources of comfort and reassurance during times of need.

Mutual Support and Reciprocity: Supporting friends and family in times of need strengthens our bonds and fosters a sense of mutual reciprocity. Knowing that we can rely on each other for support creates a sense of interdependence and solidarity that enriches our relationships and enhances our well-being.

The Value of Support from Professionals:

Expertise and Specialized Knowledge: Professionals bring expertise and specialized knowledge to help us address specific challenges or concerns. Whether it's a therapist, counselor, coach, or healthcare provider, their training and experience equip them with valuable insights and strategies to support our well-being.

Confidentiality and Non-Judgment: Professionals offer a confidential and non-judgmental space where we can express ourselves openly and honestly without fear of stigma or repercussion. Their impartiality and objectivity create a safe environment for exploring sensitive issues and working through complex emotions.

Structured Support and Guidance: Professional support often involves structured interventions and guidance tailored to our individual needs and goals. Whether it's cognitive behavioral therapy, psychoeducation, or skills training, their evidence-based approaches provide a framework for growth and change.

Accountability and Progress Monitoring: Professionals provide accountability and progress monitoring to help us stay on track with our goals and commitments. Whether it's setting milestones, tracking progress, or adjusting interventions as needed, their guidance keeps us accountable and motivated on our journey toward well-being.

Practical Strategies for Seeking Support:

Identify Your Support Network: Identify individuals in your life whom you trust and feel comfortable confiding in, whether it's friends, family members, mentors, or colleagues. Cultivate these relationships by nurturing open communication, empathy, and reciprocity.

Communicate Your Needs: Be clear and direct about your needs when seeking support, whether it's a listening ear, practical assistance, or emotional validation. Articulate your boundaries, preferences, and expectations to ensure that your needs are met respectfully and effectively.

Seek Professional Help When Needed: Don't hesitate to seek professional help from therapists, counselors, or healthcare providers when facing significant challenges or mental health concerns. Research providers who specialize in your area of need and schedule an initial consultation to assess their suitability and approach.

Explore Support Groups and Communities: Consider

joining support groups or communities that cater to your specific needs or interests, whether it's a grief support group, addiction recovery program, or online community for mental health advocacy. Connecting with others who share similar experiences can provide validation, understanding, and solidarity.

Utilize Online Resources: Take advantage of online resources, forums, and helplines that offer information, support, and guidance on a wide range of topics. Whether it's self-help articles, peer support forums, or crisis hotlines, online platforms provide accessible and anonymous support for individuals in need.

Practice Active Listening: Be an attentive and empathetic listener when supporting others, whether it's a friend, family member, or colleague. Practice active listening by offering your full attention, validating their feelings, and refraining from judgment or advice-giving unless requested.

Set Healthy Boundaries: Establish healthy boundaries in your relationships to protect your well-being and maintain balance. Communicate your limits, preferences, and expectations clearly and assertively, and respect the boundaries of others in return.

Express Gratitude and Appreciation: Show gratitude and appreciation for the support you receive from others, whether it's through a heartfelt thank you note, a kind gesture, or simply expressing your appreciation verbally. Cultivating a culture of gratitude strengthens bonds and fosters reciprocal support within your network.

Conclusion

In conclusion, seeking support from friends, family, or professionals is a valuable resource that nurtures resilience, fosters growth, and promotes overall well-being. Whether facing personal struggles, professional challenges, or mental health concerns, reaching out for support allows us to share our burdens, gain new perspectives, and access resources that empower us to cope and thrive. By cultivating meaningful relationships, communicating our needs, and seeking professional help when needed, we can build a strong support network that serves as a source of comfort, guidance, and strength on our journey through life.

9.3 Joining Support Groups or Therapy for Overthinkers: A Path to Peace of Mind

Introduction

Overthinking, characterized by persistent and repetitive thoughts, can significantly impact mental well-being, leading to anxiety, stress, and indecision. For individuals struggling with overthinking, seeking support through therapy or joining support groups can offer valuable resources and strategies to manage and overcome these challenges. In this chapter, we'll explore the benefits of joining support groups or therapy for overthinkers, how these approaches can help individuals gain insight and coping skills, and practical steps for finding the right support.

Understanding Overthinking

Overthinking is a common cognitive pattern characterized by excessive rumination, worry, and analysis of past events or future scenarios. While everyone experiences occasional bouts of overthinking, it can become problematic when it interferes with daily functioning, disrupts sleep, and exacerbates stress and anxiety. Overthinkers often find themselves trapped in a cycle of repetitive thoughts, unable to break free from negative or catastrophic thinking patterns.

The Benefits of Joining Support Groups or Therapy for Overthinkers:

Validation and Understanding: Joining support groups or therapy provides a safe and supportive environment where overthinkers can share their experiences, thoughts, and feelings without judgment. Connecting with others who share similar struggles offers validation and understanding, reducing feelings of isolation and fostering a sense of belonging.

Learning Coping Strategies: Support groups and therapy offer valuable resources and coping strategies to help overthinkers manage their symptoms more effectively. Whether it's cognitive behavioral techniques, mindfulness practices, or stress management skills, these approaches provide practical tools to interrupt negative thinking patterns and promote emotional regulation.

Gaining Insight and Perspective: Engaging in therapy or support groups allows overthinkers to gain insight into the underlying causes and triggers of their overthinking tendencies. By exploring past experiences, beliefs, and thought patterns, individuals can identify maladaptive coping mechanisms and develop healthier ways of thinking and responding to stressors.

Building Supportive Relationships: Joining support groups fosters connections with individuals who understand and empathize with the challenges of overthinking. These relationships provide a sense of camaraderie and mutual support, offering encouragement, accountability, and perspective during difficult times.

Reducing Feelings of Shame and Stigma: Overthinking can be accompanied by feelings of shame, inadequacy, or self-blame. Joining support groups or therapy helps individuals overcome these barriers by providing a safe space to express themselves openly and honestly. By normalizing their experiences and receiving validation from others, overthinkers can reduce feelings of stigma and self-judgment.

Improving Self-Esteem and Confidence: Therapy and support groups empower overthinkers to challenge negative self-talk and cultivate self-compassion and acceptance. Through guided interventions and supportive feedback, individuals can build self-esteem and confidence, recognizing their inherent worth and resilience.

Practical Steps for Joining Support Groups or Therapy for Overthinkers:

Research Available Options: Start by researching available support groups or therapy options for overthinkers in your local community or online. Look for groups or therapists specializing in anxiety, stress management, or cognitive behavioral therapy (CBT), as these approaches are particularly effective for addressing overthinking tendencies.

Ask for Recommendations: Reach out to trusted friends, family members, or healthcare providers for recommendations on support groups or therapists. Personal referrals can provide valuable insights and help you find reputable and experienced professionals who specialize in treating overthinking.

Attend a Support Group Meeting: If you're considering joining a support group, attend a meeting to get a feel for the group dynamics and see if it's a good fit for you. Pay attention to the group's atmosphere, facilitator style, and member interactions to determine if you feel comfortable and supported.

Schedule an Initial Therapy Session: If you're interested in therapy, schedule an initial session with a licensed therapist specializing in cognitive behavioral therapy or anxiety disorders. Use this session to discuss your concerns, goals, and expectations for therapy, and assess whether you feel comfortable and understood by the therapist.

Be Open and Honest: Whether participating in a support group or therapy, be open and honest about your experiences, thoughts, and feelings. Share your struggles, challenges, and goals openly with the group or therapist, and be receptive to feedback, suggestions, and support from others.

Commit to Regular Attendance: Consistency is key when participating in support groups or therapy. Commit to attending meetings or sessions regularly, even when you're feeling hesitant or discouraged. Building trust and rapport with group members or your therapist takes time, so give yourself permission to be patient and persistent.

Practice Self-Care: While engaging in support groups or therapy, prioritize self-care and wellness practices to support your overall well-being. Incorporate activities such as exercise, mindfulness, hobbies, and relaxation techniques into your daily routine to manage stress and promote emotional balance.

Set Realistic Expectations: Understand that progress in therapy or support groups may take time and effort. Set realistic expectations for yourself and be patient with the process of growth and healing. Celebrate small victories and milestones along the way, and trust in your ability to overcome challenges with time and persistence.

Conclusion

In conclusion, joining support groups or therapy for overthinkers offers valuable resources and strategies to manage and overcome the challenges associated with excessive rumination and worry. By connecting with others who share similar experiences, learning coping strategies, gaining insight and perspective, and building supportive relationships, individuals can cultivate resilience, improve self-esteem, and reduce feelings of isolation and stigma. By taking proactive steps to seek support and prioritize their mental well-being, overthinkers can embark on a journey of healing, growth, and self-discovery that leads to greater peace of mind and emotional balance.

9.4 Building Authentic Connections and Reducing Isolation: The Power of Meaningful Relationships

Introduction

In today's fast-paced and digitally-driven world, it's easy to feel disconnected and isolated despite the constant connectivity offered by technology. Many individuals struggle to build authentic connections with others, leading to feelings of loneliness, alienation, and disconnection. However, fostering meaningful relationships is essential for our mental, emotional, and physical well-being. In this chapter, we'll explore the importance of building authentic connections, the impact of social isolation on health and happiness, and practical strategies for reducing isolation and cultivating meaningful relationships.

Understanding Authentic Connections

Authentic connections are genuine, deep, and meaningful relationships that are built on trust, mutual respect, and emotional intimacy. These connections go beyond surface-level interactions and involve sharing our true selves with others, including our hopes, fears, dreams, and vulnerabilities. Authentic connections are characterized by honesty, openness, and vulnerability, allowing us to feel seen, heard, and accepted for who we truly are.

The Importance of Building Authentic Connections:

Enhanced Well-Being: Building authentic connections is essential for our mental, emotional, and physical well-being. Meaningful relationships provide emotional support, companionship, and a sense of belonging that buffer against stress, anxiety, and depression. They promote positive emotions such as joy, love, and fulfillment and contribute to overall happiness and life satisfaction.

Reduced Loneliness and Isolation: Authentic connections reduce feelings of loneliness and isolation by fostering a sense of connection and belonging. When we have supportive relationships in our lives, we feel less alone and more connected to others, even in times of adversity or hardship. This sense of belonging strengthens our resilience and promotes a sense of community and connection.

Increased Empathy and Compassion: Authentic connections cultivate empathy and compassion by encouraging us to see the world through the eyes of others. When we develop close relationships with individuals from diverse backgrounds and experiences, we gain a deeper understanding of their perspectives, challenges, and aspirations, fostering empathy and compassion for their unique journeys.

Greater Self-Awareness and Growth: Building authentic connections promotes self-awareness and personal growth by providing opportunities for reflection, feedback, and self-discovery. When we engage in meaningful relationships with others, we receive valuable insights and feedback that help us understand ourselves better, identify areas for growth, and evolve into our best selves.

Enhanced Resilience and Coping Skills: Authentic connections enhance resilience and coping skills by providing emotional support and encouragement during times of difficulty or adversity. When we have trusted individuals to whom we can turn for guidance, comfort, and reassurance, we feel better equipped to navigate life's challenges and bounce back from setbacks with strength and resilience.

The Impact of Social Isolation

Social isolation has significant negative impacts on health and well-being, both physically and mentally. Studies have linked social isolation to a range of adverse health outcomes, including increased risk of cardiovascular disease, compromised immune function, and premature mortality. Additionally, social isolation is associated with higher rates of depression, anxiety, and cognitive decline, leading to poorer mental health outcomes and decreased quality of life.

Practical Strategies for Reducing Isolation and Building Authentic Connections:

Prioritize Quality Over Quantity: Focus on building a few close, meaningful relationships rather than spreading yourself too thin with a large network of acquaintances. Invest time and effort into nurturing authentic connections with individuals who share your values, interests, and aspirations.

Be Authentic and Vulnerable: Be authentic and vulnerable in your interactions with others, sharing your true thoughts, feelings, and experiences openly and honestly. Allow yourself to be seen and heard for who you truly are, and encourage others to do the same. Authenticity fosters trust, intimacy, and connection in relationships.

Listen with Empathy: Practice active listening and empathy in your interactions with others, seeking to understand their perspectives, feelings, and experiences without judgment or interruption. Validate their emotions and experiences, and offer support and encouragement as needed. Listening with empathy strengthens bonds and deepens connections with others.

Engage in Meaningful Activities: Engage in activities and pursuits that align with your interests, values, and passions, and seek out opportunities to connect with others who share your enthusiasm. Whether it's joining a book club, volunteering for a cause you care about, or participating in a hobby group, engaging in meaningful activities facilitates connections with like-minded individuals.

Use Technology Mindfully: While technology can facilitate connection and communication, it's essential to use it mindfully and intentionally. Limit screen time and prioritize face-to-face interactions whenever possible. Use technology as a tool for maintaining connections with distant friends and family members, but prioritize in-person interactions for building deeper, more meaningful relationships.

Practice Gratitude and Appreciation: Cultivate a mindset of gratitude and appreciation for the relationships and connections in your life. Take time to express gratitude and appreciation for the people who support and uplift you, whether it's through a heartfelt thank you note, a kind gesture, or simply expressing your appreciation verbally. Gratitude strengthens bonds and fosters reciprocal support in relationships.

Seek Support When Needed: Don't hesitate to seek support from friends, family, or professionals when you're feeling overwhelmed, stressed, or lonely. Reach out to trusted individuals for emotional support, companionship, and encouragement, and consider seeking therapy or counseling if you're struggling with mental health concerns. Seeking support is a sign of strength, not weakness, and it's essential for maintaining well-being and resilience.

Be Proactive in Building Connections: Take initiative in building connections with others by initiating conversations, making plans, and reaching out to new people. Attend social events, networking opportunities, and community gatherings where you can meet new people and expand your social circle. Building connections requires effort and initiative, so be proactive in seeking out opportunities for meaningful interaction and connection.

Conclusion

In conclusion, building authentic connections and reducing isolation is essential for our mental, emotional, and physical well-being. Meaningful relationships provide emotional support, companionship, and a sense of belonging that promote resilience, happiness, and overall quality of life.

10.1 Taking Action and Moving Forward: Empowering Steps Toward Growth and Fulfillment

Introduction

Chapter 10 marks a crucial turning point in our journey toward personal growth and fulfillment. It's the chapter where we transition from contemplation to action, from reflection to implementation. Taking action requires courage, commitment, and resilience as we embark on the path toward realizing our goals and aspirations. In this chapter, we'll explore the empowering steps we can take to move forward, overcome obstacles, and create a life filled with purpose, meaning, and fulfillment.

Embracing the Power of Action:

Turning Intentions into Action: Intentions are the seeds of change, but action is the water that nourishes them to fruition. While introspection and reflection are essential, they must be accompanied by decisive action to effect meaningful change in our lives. Taking action empowers us to move beyond the confines of our comfort zones and step into the realm of possibility and growth.

Overcoming Procrastination: Procrastination is the enemy of progress, often fueled by fear, self-doubt, or perfectionism. By taking decisive action and breaking tasks into manageable steps, we can overcome procrastination and build momentum toward our goals. Each small step forward contributes to our sense of accomplishment and motivates us to keep moving forward.

Cultivating Resilience: Taking action requires resilience—the ability to bounce back from setbacks and persevere in the face of challenges. By cultivating resilience, we develop the inner strength and determination to overcome obstacles and stay focused on our goals, even when the journey becomes difficult. Resilience enables us to view setbacks as opportunities for growth and learning rather than insurmountable barriers.

Setting Clear Goals and Intentions:

Defining Your Vision: Clarify your vision for the future by identifying your values, passions, and aspirations. What do you truly want to achieve in life? What kind of person do you want to become? Setting a clear vision provides direction and purpose, guiding your actions and decisions as you move forward.

Setting SMART Goals: Transform your vision into actionable goals by setting SMART goals—specific, measurable, achievable, relevant, and time-bound. Break down your goals into smaller, manageable tasks, and establish a timeline for completion. SMART goals provide a roadmap for success, helping you stay focused and accountable as you work toward your aspirations.

Creating a Vision Board: Visualize your goals and aspirations by creating a vision board—a visual representation of your dreams and desires. Gather images, quotes, and symbols that resonate with your vision and arrange them on a board or canvas. Place your vision board in a prominent location where you'll see it daily, serving as a reminder of your goals and motivating you to take action.

Taking Consistent Action Toward Your Goals:

Developing an Action Plan: Create an action plan outlining the specific steps you'll take to achieve your goals. Break down each goal into actionable tasks and prioritize them based on importance and urgency. Establish a daily or weekly routine that includes dedicated time for working toward your goals, and commit to following through consistently.

Practicing Discipline and Accountability: Cultivate discipline and accountability by setting clear expectations for yourself and holding yourself to high standards. Stay committed to your action plan, even when faced with distractions or obstacles. Consider enlisting an accountability partner—a friend, family member, or mentor—who can support and encourage you in your journey.

Celebrating Progress: Celebrate your progress and achievements along the way, no matter how small. Acknowledge the effort and dedication you've invested in pursuing your goals, and reward yourself for reaching milestones. Celebrating progress boosts your confidence and motivation, fueling your drive to continue moving forward.

Embracing Adaptability and Flexibility:

Navigating Uncertainty: Embrace uncertainty as an inherent part of the journey toward growth and fulfillment. Life is unpredictable, and obstacles and setbacks are inevitable. Instead of resisting change, embrace it as an opportunity for learning and adaptation. Stay flexible and open-minded, and be willing to adjust your plans as needed in response to new information or circumstances.

Learning from Setbacks: View setbacks as valuable learning experiences that offer insights and lessons for growth. When faced with obstacles or failures, take time to reflect on what went wrong and identify opportunities for improvement. Use setbacks as motivation to refine your approach, strengthen your resilience, and continue moving forward with renewed determination.

Seeking Support and Collaboration:

Building a Support Network: Surround yourself with a supportive network of friends, family members, mentors, and peers who believe in your vision and encourage your growth. Seek guidance, feedback, and encouragement from those who have walked a similar path or possess valuable expertise and experience. A strong support network provides encouragement, accountability, and perspective, empowering you to overcome challenges and stay focused on your goals.

Collaborating with Others: Collaboration fosters innovation, creativity, and mutual growth by bringing together diverse perspectives and talents. Look for opportunities to collaborate with others who share your values and goals, whether it's through joint projects, mastermind groups, or mentorship relationships. Collaborative partnerships provide a platform for sharing ideas, resources, and support, accelerating your progress and amplifying your impact.

Practicing Self-Compassion and Self-Care:

Cultivating Self-Compassion: Be kind and compassionate toward yourself, especially in moments of difficulty or self-doubt. Acknowledge your strengths, accomplishments, and progress, and treat yourself with the same empathy and understanding you would offer to a friend. Practice self-compassion by embracing imperfection, learning from mistakes, and nurturing a positive self-image.

Prioritizing Self-Care: Prioritize self-care as an essential component of your journey toward growth and fulfillment. Take time to nourish your body, mind, and spirit through activities that replenish your energy and restore balance. Whether it's exercise, meditation, hobbies, or spending time in nature, prioritize activities that bring you joy, relaxation, and inner peace. Remember that self-care is not selfish—it's a necessary investment in your well-being that enables you to show up fully in pursuit of your goals and aspirations.

Conclusion

In conclusion, taking action and moving forward is the pivotal step that transforms our dreams and aspirations into reality. By setting clear goals, developing actionable plans, and taking consistent steps toward our vision, we empower ourselves to create a life filled with purpose, meaning, and fulfillment. Embrace the journey with courage, resilience, and determination, knowing that each step forward brings you closer to your goals and aspirations. Remember that progress is not always linear, and setbacks are opportunities for growth and learning. By embracing adaptability, seeking support and collaboration, and practicing self-compassion and self-care, you'll navigate the ups and downs of the journey with grace and resilience. Trust in your abilities, stay focused on your vision, and take action and move forward.

10.2 Developing an Action Plan to Overcome Overthinking: Practical Strategies for Cultivating Clarity and Peace of Mind

Introduction

Overthinking can be a debilitating pattern of thought that traps us in a cycle of rumination, worry, and indecision. It not only hampers our productivity and creativity but also takes a toll on our mental and emotional well-being. However, overcoming overthinking is possible with the right mindset and strategies. In this chapter, we'll delve into the development of an action plan to overcome overthinking, offering practical strategies and techniques to cultivate clarity, peace of mind, and a more balanced approach to thinking.

Identifying Overthinking Patterns: The first step in overcoming overthinking is to recognize and understand the patterns of thought that contribute to it. Overthinking often involves repetitive and intrusive thoughts, excessive worry about past or future events, and a tendency to dwell on negative outcomes or scenarios. By becoming aware of these patterns, we can begin to challenge and change them.

Exploring the Root Causes: Overthinking can stem from various underlying factors, including perfectionism, fear of failure, low self-esteem, or anxiety. It's essential to explore the root causes of our overthinking tendencies to address them effectively. Reflecting on past experiences, childhood conditioning, and core beliefs can provide insights into the origins of our overthinking patterns.

Developing an Action Plan:

Setting Clear Objectives: Define clear objectives for overcoming overthinking, such as reducing rumination, improving decision-making skills, or cultivating a more positive mindset. Having specific goals gives direction and purpose to our efforts and allows us to track our progress effectively.

Identifying Triggering Situations: Identify situations or circumstances that trigger overthinking tendencies, such as stressful deadlines, social interactions, or uncertainty about the future. Recognizing these triggers enables us to prepare and implement strategies to manage them proactively.

Practicing Mindfulness and Awareness: Cultivate mindfulness and self-awareness as foundational skills for overcoming overthinking. Mindfulness involves paying attention to the present moment without judgment, allowing us to observe our thoughts and emotions objectively. By practicing mindfulness techniques such as meditation, deep breathing, or body scanning, we can develop greater clarity and presence of the mind.

Implementing Thought Monitoring: Implement a thought monitoring practice to track and analyze overthinking patterns. Keep a journal or use a mental health app to record instances of overthinking, including the triggering events, the content of the thoughts, and the associated emotions. This practice helps us identify recurring themes and patterns, making it easier to intervene and challenge them effectively.

Challenging Negative Thought Patterns: Challenge negative thought patterns and cognitive distortions that fuel overthinking, such as catastrophizing, black-and-white thinking, or mind reading. Use cognitive behavioral techniques to question the accuracy and validity of these thoughts, replacing them with more balanced and rational alternatives. Practice reframing negative thoughts into more constructive and empowering perspectives.

Setting Boundaries with Rumination: Establish boundaries with rumination by setting aside dedicated time for reflection and problem-solving. Designate a specific period each day to address concerns or worries, allowing yourself to explore them in a structured and productive manner. Outside of this designated time, practice redirecting your attention to the present moment and engaging in activities that promote relaxation and enjoyment.

Engaging in Problem-Solving: Develop effective problem-solving skills to address the underlying issues that contribute to overthinking. Break down complex problems into manageable steps, brainstorm potential solutions, and weigh the pros and cons of each option. Focus on identifying actionable steps that you can take to address the problem rather than getting bogged down by hypothetical scenarios or worst-case outcomes.

Practicing Acceptance and Letting Go: Cultivate acceptance and letting go as essential components of overcoming overthinking. Acceptance involves acknowledging and embracing the present moment as it is, without resistance or judgment. Letting go entails releasing attachment to outcomes and relinquishing control over situations beyond our influence. By practicing acceptance and letting go, we free ourselves from the grip of overthinking and open ourselves to the possibilities of the present moment.

Seeking Support and Guidance: Don't hesitate to seek support and guidance from trusted friends, family members, or mental health professionals. Share your struggles and challenges with others who can offer empathy, perspective, and encouragement. Consider seeking therapy or counseling to explore deeper-rooted issues and develop personalized strategies for overcoming overthinking.

Celebrating Progress and Success: Celebrate your progress and successes along the way, no matter how small. Acknowledge the efforts you've invested in overcoming overthinking and recognize the positive changes you've made in your thinking patterns and behaviors. Celebrating progress boosts confidence and motivation, reinforcing your commitment to continued growth and development.

Implementing the Action Plan:

Commitment and Consistency: Commit to implementing the action plan with consistency and dedication. Overcoming overthinking requires ongoing effort and practice, so stay committed to your goals even when faced with challenges or setbacks. Be patient and compassionate with yourself as you navigate the process of change and growth.

Flexibility and Adaptation: Stay flexible and adaptable in your approach, adjusting your strategies as needed based on feedback and results. What works for one person may not work for another, so be willing to experiment with different techniques and tailor them to your unique needs and preferences.

Reflection and Adjustment: Regularly reflect on your progress and experiences, identifying areas of improvement and areas of strength. Use feedback from your thought monitoring practice and self-reflection to adjust your action plan and refine your strategies over time. Remember that personal growth is a journey, not a destination, so embrace the process of continuous learning and evolution.

Seeking Support and Accountability: Lean on your support network for encouragement, guidance, and accountability. Share your goals and progress with trusted individuals who can offer support and hold you accountable to your commitments. Consider joining a support group or finding an accountability partner who shares similar goals and can provide mutual encouragement and motivation.

Conclusion

In conclusion, developing an action plan to overcome overthinking is a proactive and empowering process that requires self-awareness, commitment, and resilience. By setting clear objectives, identifying triggering situations, and implementing practical strategies, we can cultivate clarity, peace of mind, and a more balanced approach to thinking. Remember that overcoming overthinking is a journey, not a destination, so be patient and compassionate with yourself as you navigate the ups and downs of the process. With dedication and perseverance, you can break free from the grip of overthinking and create a life filled with clarity, purpose, and fulfillment.

10.3 Setting Achievable Goals and Celebrating Progress: Keys to Sustainable Growth and Motivation

Introduction

Setting achievable goals and celebrating progress are essential components of personal growth and success.

Goals provide direction and purpose, motivating us to take action and pursue our aspirations. However, setting unrealistic goals can lead to frustration and burnout, undermining our confidence and motivation. By setting achievable goals and celebrating progress, we create a positive feedback loop that sustains momentum and fosters a sense of accomplishment. In this chapter, we'll explore the importance of setting achievable goals, practical strategies for goal setting, and the value of celebrating progress along the way.

Understanding Achievable Goals:

Clarity and Specificity: Achievable goals are clear, specific, and well-defined, allowing us to focus our efforts and resources effectively. Rather than setting vague or ambiguous goals, such as "improve fitness" or "get better at work," break them down into concrete and actionable objectives, such as "run a 5k race" or "complete a professional certification."

Realistic and Attainable: Achievable goals are realistic and attainable within a reasonable timeframe, considering our current abilities, resources, and constraints. While it's important to challenge ourselves and strive for growth, setting goals that are overly ambitious or beyond our capabilities can set us up for failure and demotivation.

Relevance and Alignment: Achievable goals are relevant and aligned with our values, priorities, and long-term objectives. They reflect what truly matters to us and contribute to our overall sense of fulfillment and well-being. Aligning goals with our intrinsic motivations increases our commitment and resilience in pursuing them.

Practical Strategies for Goal Setting:

SMART Goals Framework: Use the SMART goals framework to set achievable goals that are Specific, Measurable, Achievable, Relevant, and Time-bound. Break down large goals into smaller, more manageable tasks, and establish clear criteria for success and progress tracking. For example, instead of setting a vague goal to "read more books," set a SMART goal to "read one book per month for the next six months."

Chunking and Sequencing: Break down complex goals into smaller, bite-sized tasks or milestones, known as chunking. By dividing goals into manageable chunks, we reduce getting overwhelmed and increase clarity and focus. Sequencing involves arranging tasks in a logical order that maximizes efficiency and progress. Prioritize tasks based on urgency, importance, or dependency, ensuring a smooth progression toward the ultimate goal.

Prioritization and Focus: Prioritize goals based on their significance, impact, and alignment with your overall objectives. Focus your time, energy, and resources on high-priority goals that have the greatest potential to move you closer to your desired outcomes. Avoid spreading yourself too thin by setting too many goals simultaneously, as this can dilute your efforts and hinder progress.

Accountability and Commitment: Hold yourself accountable to your goals by establishing clear commitments and deadlines. Share your goals with trusted friends, family members, or mentors who can offer support, encouragement, and accountability. Consider joining a mastermind group or finding an accountability partner who shares similar goals and can provide mutual motivation and support.

The Value of Celebrating Progress:

Boosting Motivation and Confidence: Celebrating progress boosts motivation and confidence by acknowledging and reinforcing our achievements along the way. When we celebrate small wins and milestones, we experience a sense of accomplishment and validation that fuels our momentum and resilience. This positive reinforcement strengthens our belief in our abilities and motivates us to continue pursuing our goals with enthusiasm and determination.

Cultivating Gratitude and Satisfaction: Celebrating progress cultivates gratitude and satisfaction by fostering an appreciation for the journey and the effort invested in pursuing our goals. It shifts our focus from the destination to the process, allowing us to savor the moments of growth, learning, and self-discovery along the way. By acknowledging our progress, we cultivate a sense of fulfillment and contentment that transcends external achievements.

Enhancing Resilience and Perseverance: Celebrating progress enhances resilience and perseverance by providing encouragement and validation during challenging times. When we encounter setbacks or obstacles, reflecting on our past successes and milestones reminds us of our resilience and capacity to overcome adversity. This resilience mindset enables us to bounce back stronger and more determined to continue pursuing our goals, regardless of the challenges we may face.

Practical Strategies for Celebrating Progress:

Acknowledge Achievements: Take time to acknowledge and celebrate your achievements, no matter how small. Whether it's reaching a milestone, completing a task, or making progress toward a goal, pause to recognize and appreciate your efforts and accomplishments. Acknowledge the skills, strengths, and qualities that enabled you to succeed, and express gratitude for the support and resources that contributed to your progress.

Reward Yourself: Reward yourself for reaching milestones and achieving goals by treating yourself to something special or engaging in activities that bring you joy and relaxation. Whether it's indulging in your favorite meal, taking a day off to rest and recharge, or treating yourself to a meaningful experience, rewards provide positive reinforcement and motivation to continue moving forward.

Share Successes: Share your successes and milestones with others who have supported and encouraged you along the way. Whether it's sharing a progress update with friends, family members, or colleagues or posting about your achievements on social media, sharing successes allows you to celebrate with others and receive validation and encouragement from your support network.

Reflect on Progress: Take time to reflect on your progress and growth periodically, reviewing your achievements and milestones over time. Reflective practices such as journaling, meditation, or self-assessment allow you to gain perspective on your journey, identify areas of growth and improvement, and celebrate how far you've come since you started. Use this reflection as fuel to propel you forward toward new goals and aspirations.

Overcoming Challenges and Staying Motivated:

Navigating Setbacks: Embrace setbacks and challenges as opportunities for growth and learning rather than obstacles to success. When faced with setbacks, reflect on the lessons learned and identify opportunities for improvement or adjustment. Use setbacks as motivation to reassess your goals, refine your strategies, and recommit to your journey with renewed determination.

Maintaining Momentum: Maintain momentum by staying focused on your goals and taking consistent action toward their achievement. Break goals down into smaller, manageable tasks, and establish a routine or schedule that supports progress. Stay flexible and adaptable in your approach, adjusting your strategies as needed to overcome obstacles and stay on track.

Seeking Support: Seek support from friends, family members, or mentors during challenging times, leveraging their encouragement, guidance, and perspective. Don't hesitate to ask for help or seek advice when needed, as sharing your challenges with others can provide valuable insights and support. Surround yourself with individuals who believe in your potential and are invested in your success.

Conclusion

In conclusion, setting achievable goals and celebrating progress are integral components of personal growth, motivation, and success. By setting clear, realistic goals and implementing practical strategies for goal setting, we create a roadmap for success that guides our actions and priorities. Celebrating progress along the way boosts motivation, confidence, and resilience, reinforcing our commitment to continued growth and development. Remember to acknowledge your achievements, cultivate gratitude and satisfaction, and share successes with others who have supported and encouraged you. Stay resilient in the face of challenges, maintain momentum through consistent action, and seek support when needed to overcome obstacles and stay focused on your journey toward success. With dedication, perseverance, and a celebration of progress, you can achieve your goals and create a life filled with purpose, fulfillment, and meaning.

10.4 Nurturing Mindfulness and Self-Awareness: Keys to Flourishing in the Journey Ahead

Introduction

As we embark on our journey of growth and self-discovery, maintaining mindfulness and self-awareness is paramount. Mindfulness—the practice of being present and attentive to our thoughts, feelings, and experiences—cultivates a deeper connection with ourselves and the world around us. Similarly, self-awareness—the ability to recognize and understand our thoughts, emotions, and behaviors—empowers us to make conscious choices and navigate life's challenges with clarity and resilience. In this chapter, we'll explore the importance of nurturing mindfulness and self-awareness in our journey ahead, practical strategies for cultivating these qualities, and their transformative impact on our well-being and personal growth.

Understanding Mindfulness and Self-Awareness:

Mindfulness: Mindfulness is the practice of bringing intentional awareness to the present moment without judgment or attachment. It involves tuning into our thoughts, sensations, and emotions with curiosity and openness, allowing us to experience life more fully and authentically. Mindfulness enables us to cultivate presence, acceptance, and compassion toward ourselves and others, fostering inner peace and resilience in the face of life's challenges.

Self-awareness: Self-awareness is the ability to observe and understand our thoughts, emotions, and behaviors objectively. It involves recognizing our strengths, weaknesses, values, and motivations, as well as how they influence our actions and decisions. Self-awareness empowers us to take ownership of our lives, identify areas for growth and improvement, and make intentional choices aligned with our values and aspirations.

The Importance of Maintaining Mindfulness and Self-Awareness:

Enhanced Well-Being: Maintaining mindfulness and self-awareness enhances our overall well-being by promoting mental clarity, emotional resilience, and inner peace. Mindfulness practices such as meditation, deep breathing, or body scanning reduce stress, anxiety, and depression while increasing feelings of calmness, relaxation, and contentment. Self-awareness fosters a deeper understanding of our needs, boundaries, and priorities, enabling us to cultivate healthier relationships and lifestyles.

Improved Decision-Making: Mindfulness and self-awareness improve our decision-making skills by helping us make choices aligned with our values, goals, and priorities. By tuning into our thoughts, emotions, and intuition, we gain clarity and insight into the consequences of our actions, allowing us to make informed and intentional decisions. Self-awareness enables us to recognize and overcome biases, limiting beliefs, and habitual patterns of behavior that may impede our judgment or hinder our progress.

Effective Stress Management: Maintaining mindfulness and self-awareness is essential for effective stress management, enabling us to navigate life's challenges with grace and resilience. Mindfulness practices provide coping mechanisms for managing stressors such as work pressures, relationship conflicts, or health concerns, reducing physiological arousal and promoting emotional regulation.

Self-awareness allows us to identify stress triggers, recognize early warning signs of burnout, and implement proactive strategies for self-care and stress reduction.

Enhanced Relationships: Mindfulness and self-awareness enhance the quality of our relationships by fostering empathy, communication, and connection. By cultivating present-moment awareness and non-judgmental listening, we create space for authentic and meaningful interactions with others, deepening our understanding and appreciation of their perspectives and experiences. Self-awareness promotes self-compassion and empathy, enabling us to relate to others with greater compassion, empathy, and understanding.

Practical Strategies for Nurturing Mindfulness and Self-Awareness:

Mindfulness Meditation: Incorporate mindfulness meditation into your daily routine to cultivate present-moment awareness and inner peace. Set aside dedicated time each day for meditation practice, starting with short sessions and gradually increasing the duration as you build consistency and comfort. Focus on observing your breath, bodily sensations, or mental processes without judgment, allowing thoughts to come and go with gentleness and acceptance.

Mindful Movement: Engage in mindful movement practices such as yoga, tai chi, or qigong to integrate mindfulness into your physical activity. Pay attention to the sensations, rhythm, and alignment of your body as you move through various poses or sequences, connecting with the present moment and cultivating a sense of embodied awareness. Mindful movement promotes relaxation, flexibility, and balance while reducing tension and stress in the body and mind.

Daily Reflection: Set aside time each day for reflection and self-inquiry to deepen your self-awareness and understanding. Journaling, contemplative writing, or guided self-reflection exercises can provide a structured framework for exploring your thoughts, emotions, and experiences. Reflect on your achievements, challenges, and insights, identifying patterns and themes that offer valuable insights into your inner landscape and personal growth journey.

Sensory Awareness: Practice sensory awareness exercises to anchor yourself in the present moment and cultivate mindfulness in everyday activities. Engage your senses by noticing the sights, sounds, smells, tastes, and textures around you with curiosity and appreciation. Whether you're walking in nature, eating a meal, or taking a shower, immerse yourself fully in the sensory experience, allowing it to ground you in the here and now.

Mindful Communication: Practice mindful communication in your interactions with others, focusing on active listening, empathy, and non-judgmental presence. Pay attention to the words, tone, and body language of the person you're communicating with, tuning into their needs, emotions, and perspectives with openness and compassion. Pause before responding, allowing space for reflection and intentionality in your communication.

Integrating Mindfulness and Self-Awareness into Daily Life:

Morning Rituals: Start your day with a mindfulness ritual such as meditation, gratitude practice, or mindful movement to set a positive tone for the day ahead. Create a sacred space or sanctuary where you can engage in these practices with intention and presence, nourishing your mind, body, and spirit before diving into the demands of daily life.

Mindful Moments: Infuse mindfulness into everyday activities by incorporating mindful moments throughout your day. Pause periodically to check in with yourself, take a few deep breaths, and reconnect with the present moment. Whether you're washing dishes, commuting to work, or waiting in line, use these moments as opportunities to cultivate mindfulness and self-awareness in the midst of your busy schedule.

Evening Reflection: End your day with an evening reflection practice to review your experiences, insights, and lessons learned. Journal about your day, acknowledging your achievements, challenges, and areas for growth with honesty and compassion. Celebrate your successes and express gratitude for the blessings in your life, cultivating a sense of fulfillment and contentment as you prepare for rest and rejuvenation.

Bedtime Routine: Create a bedtime routine that promotes relaxation and mindfulness, preparing your body and mind for restful sleep. Engage in calming activities such as gentle stretching, reading, or listening to soothing music to unwind from the day's stressors. Practice relaxation techniques such as progressive muscle relaxation or guided imagery to release tension and quiet the mind, facilitating a peaceful transition into sleep.

Overcoming Challenges and Sustaining Practice:

Cultivating Patience and Persistence: Cultivate patience and persistence in your mindfulness and self-awareness practice, recognizing that it's a journey of continuous growth and refinement. Be gentle and compassionate with yourself, allowing for moments of struggle, resistance, and doubt without judgment or self-criticism. Trust in the process of transformation, knowing that every moment of mindfulness and self-awareness brings you closer to your true essence and potential.

Navigating Distractions and Resistance: Recognize and navigate distractions and resistance that may arise in your mindfulness and self-awareness practice. Whether it's internal distractions such as wandering thoughts or external distractions such as noise or interruptions, gently guide your attention back to the present moment with patience and persistence. Notice resistance or discomfort that arises during mindfulness practice and explore it with curiosity and compassion, recognizing it as an opportunity for growth and insight.

Seeking Support and Community: Seek support and community in your mindfulness and self-awareness journey by connecting with like-minded individuals or joining mindfulness groups or classes. Surround yourself with a supportive network of friends, family members, or mentors who share your values and aspirations, providing encouragement, accountability, and camaraderie along the way. Share your experiences, insights, and challenges with others who can offer empathy, validation, and guidance, fostering a sense of belonging and connection in your practice.

Conclusion

In conclusion, maintaining mindfulness and self-awareness is essential for flourishing in the journey ahead, empowering us to navigate life's complexities with clarity, compassion, and resilience. By nurturing present-moment awareness and self-understanding, we cultivate inner peace, authenticity, and well-being, enhancing our relationships, decision-making, and overall quality of life. Through mindfulness practices such as meditation, mindful movement, and sensory awareness, we anchor ourselves in the present moment and deepen our connection with ourselves and the world around us.

By integrating mindfulness and self-awareness into our daily routines and rituals, we create a foundation for sustainable growth and transformation, embracing each moment as an opportunity for learning, growth, and self-discovery. With patience, persistence, and an open heart, we embark on the journey ahead with courage, curiosity, and gratitude, trusting in the transformative power of mindfulness and self-awareness to illuminate our path and illuminate our path and lead us toward greater fulfillment and purpose.

The Final Conclusion

As we reach the culmination of our exploration into overcoming overthinking, we find ourselves at the threshold of transformation, poised to embrace the path to freedom and self-discovery. Reflecting on the journey thus far, we've traversed the intricate labyrinth of our minds, unraveling the knots of doubt, fear, and uncertainty that once bound us. Through introspection, self-awareness, and resilience, we've navigated the twists and turns of our inner landscape, illuminating the shadows of overthinking with the light of mindfulness and compassion.

The path to freedom from overthinking is not linear nor without its challenges. It's a journey marked by moments of clarity and confusion, progress and setbacks, triumphs and trials. Yet, with each step forward, we reclaim a piece of ourselves, reclaiming our power to choose presence over rumination, acceptance over resistance, and courage over fear. As we stand on the precipice of possibility, we are reminded of the profound wisdom inherent in the practice of self-care and mindfulness.

In the hustle and bustle of modern life, it's easy to lose sight of the importance of self-care and mindfulness. Yet, it is in these moments of quiet reflection and gentle self-nurturing that we replenish our spirits, recharge our energies, and realign with our true selves. Just as a gardener tends to their garden with care and attention, so too must we tend to the garden of our minds, cultivating seeds of peace, joy, and resilience.

As we conclude our journey of overcoming overthinking,

let us carry forth the torch of self-care and mindfulness with renewed dedication and commitment. Let us continue to nurture our minds, bodies, and spirits with kindness, compassion, and grace, knowing that each moment of self-care is an act of radical self-love and liberation. Let us embrace the journey of personal growth and resilience with open hearts and open minds, trusting in our innate capacity to rise above adversity and thrive in the face of uncertainty.

In the words of Rumi, "The wound is the place where the light enters you." May we embrace our wounds as gateways to healing and transformation, embracing the light of awareness and acceptance that illuminates our path. As we bid farewell to the shadows of overthinking, let us step boldly into the brilliance of our authentic selves, knowing that the journey of self-discovery is endless and ever-unfolding.

References

- Kabat-Zinn, J. (1994). Wherever you go, there you are: Mindfulness meditation in everyday life. Hachette Books
- Siegel, D. J. (2010). The mindful brain: Reflection and attunement in the cultivation of well-being. WW Norton & Company.
- Brown, B. (2010). The gifts of imperfection: Let go of who you think you're supposed to be and embrace who you are. Hazelden Publishing.
- Hayes, S. C., Strosahl, K. D., & Wilson, K. G. (2011). Acceptance and commitment therapy: The process and practice of mindful change. Guilford Press.
- Harris, R. (2009). ACT made simple: An easy-to-read primer on acceptance and commitment therapy. New Harbinger Publications.
- Dweck, C. S. (2006). Mindset: The new psychology of success. Ballantine Books.
- Kabat-Zinn, J. (2005). Full catastrophe living: Using the wisdom of your body and mind to face stress, pain, and illness. Delta.
- Epstein, M. (2018). Advice Not Given: A Guide to Getting Over Yourself. Penguin.
- Chödrön, P. (2009). The places that scare you: A guide to fearlessness in difficult times. Shambhala Publications.
- Germer, C. K. (2009). The mindful path to self-compassion: Freeing yourself from destructive thoughts and emotions. Guilford Press.
- Neff, K. D. (2011). Self-compassion: Stop beating

yourself up and leave insecurity behind. HarperCollins.

- Thich Nhat Hanh. (1991). Peace Is Every Step: The Path of Mindfulness in Everyday Life. Bantam.
- Langer, E. J. (2014). Mindfulness. Da Capo Lifelong Books.
- Bishop, S. R., Lau, M., Shapiro, S., Carlson, L., Anderson, N. D., Carmody, J.,... & Devins, G. (2004). Mindfulness: A proposed operational definition. Clinical Psychology: Science and Practice, 11(3), 230-241
- Goleman, D., & Davidson, R. J. (2017). Altered Traits: Science Reveals How Meditation Changes Your Mind, Brain, and Body. Penguin.
- Creswell, J. D. (2017). Mindfulness interventions. Annual Review of Psychology, 68, 491-516.
- Grossman, P., Niemann, L., Schmidt, S., & Walach, H. (2004). Mindfulness-based stress reduction and health benefits: A meta-analysis. Journal of Psychosomatic Research, 57(1), 35-43.
- Shapiro, S. L., Brown, K. W., & Astin, J. (2011). Toward the integration of meditation into higher education: A review of research evidence. Teachers College Record, 113(3), 493-528.
- Baer, R. A. (2003). Mindfulness training as a clinical intervention: A conceptual and empirical review. Clinical Psychology: Science and Practice, 10(2), 125-143.
- Segal, Z. V., Williams, J. M. G., & Teasdale, J. D. (2018). Mindfulness-Based Cognitive Therapy for Depression, Second Edition. Guilford Publications.

9 7 9 8 8 9 4 9 8 0 2 8 7